A Mighty Tree

By

Rev. David E. Clarke

Copyright 2015
By
Rev. David E. Clarke

ISBN 978-1-940609-26-3
Softcover

The Bible used in this book is from the NKJV.

This book was printed in the United States of America.

To order additional copies of this book, contact:

Rev. David E. Clarke
P.O. 82
Ashville, Ohio 43103

Published by FWB Publications
Columbus, Ohio

FWB

Rev. David E. Clarke

DEDICATION

This book is dedicated to my brother and sister-in-law Len and Linda Clarke for their continuing friendship and love and their many ways and means they have helped a person like me through this life.

This book is also dedicated in loving memory to my Father and Mother, my family, friends, and foremost to my Lord:

Ho Kurios Mou Kai Ho Theos Mou

ACKNOWLEDGEMENTS

There are so many I need to acknowledge due this work and my life in general. I can only try to thank a few in this short paragraph, but to all in my life, I am thankful.

I need to thank Mr. Timothy Perkins for his years of friendship and support. He as always has been a friend and brother to me.

To those in membership at the Williamsport Community Lighthouse Church and the First Church of Christ in Christian Union Church and especially Brother Larry Keller's Sunday School Class. Thank you all so much.

My many thanks and appreciations are given, as always to my publisher and friend, Dr. Alton Loveless.

PREFACE

"A Mighty Tree," is a short work attempting to explore the Christian life of a believer. It is offered in two parts. The first is a dream allegory. For many years, I have had a mental image of the Christian life symbolized as a tree.

I have used the allegory also to recognize certain important people of my life. They were my mentors and I have included them as my guides in this work.

The first of my guides is Professor Clive Staples Lewis of Oxford and Cambridge. I, like so many others, have been influenced and mentored in his writings and profoundness of his Christian belief and advocacy.

The second is my father, Mr. Charles Kenith Clarke. He was a scholar though he never attended any university. We would discuss and argue a vast range of topics including the Bible and Christian doctrine. I do so miss this time with him.

A third mentor was Dr. Ora Lovell. We would travel around together and listened to each other speak. We would spend hours at restaurants tying up a table discussing various Greek New Testament passages or theological points of view.

My fourth mentor found within this work is Rev. Joseph Johnson. He retired as a pastor within the Churches of Christ in Christian Union and while at the age of 70 became the pastor of the Inner City Ministries. I was honored to have worked with him at that facility. He finally retired from the Mission at the age of 94.

All of the above have passed into eternity, but I have one remaining mentor and teacher left here to guide me. He is Dr. Alton Loveless. He is my publisher and friend.

There is an additional mentor that I have been blessed to have had. She was Dr. Erika Bourguignon of the Ohio State University. While a student there I was honored to have sat in different classes that she taught. She taught me to think in different ways and directions. I felt I needed to mention her as she also has passed this past February, 2015.

The second part of this work is a narrative of a sermon I gave at the Williamsport Community Lighthouse Church in Williamsport, Ohio. The sermon concerned the same topic and I thought it was good to come at the topic from a secondary perspective and method.

This work is my attempt to try and help other believers understand a bit more concerning the Christian life. I offer this work to glorify the Lord as I try to explain in a very limited way and mortal fashion the endless and matchless grace offered by the God of the universe in redeeming fallen man back unto Himself.

TABLE OF CONTENTS

A MIGHTY TREE – THE DREAM

----------The Storm --------

I awoke from my deep slumber. I shivered being uncovered from the blanket due the cold of the damp dark night. I gazed about my drafty old bedroom seeing only the darkness of the early morning and the shocking occasional light of the lightning from a storm far away in the distance displayed through my bedroom window. The pelting of heavy rain hit the window panes. The storm called in its deep baritone roar and had awakened me. The noise of the tumult had jerked me from my sleep, but something was wrong. Something was different. I felt a fear. I felt a giant fear of an unreal nature. I was too old to fear such a fear. It was one much like a child would have down deep. I was a man and certainly was not a child. I was full grown.

I felt so clammy and wet not from any certain ague of a cold or influenza, but due an embodying sense of something not quite right in my heart or mind or soul. The perspiration rolled down my brow and over my face. My heart was beating and it seemed it would explode within my chest. The fear I had never felt before surrounded and engulfed me with intensity so great that in that strange moment I felt death. Another lightning bolt blazed across the sky outside my room. I peered through my torment around and about the room. There was nothing unusual there to see, but that which should be there. I was alone, so very alone. I could not understand what or who had roused me from my deep sleep. But something or someone had and that presence remained.

I jerked up and set on the edge of my bed. I reached for my robe that was straddled upon my sitting chair close by the bed. I used the sleeve of the robe and wiped my brow and face. I felt some comfort from this act. My fears abated a tad. My concerns waned a bit. I looked again through the darkness about the room and saw nothing out of sorts. Did my fear arise from a nightmare? Nightmares are so weird. They can come from who knows where and take a person through some surreal passages into strange caves of a psychological and inner world that to a conscience mind did not seem to make any sense. They take on a life of their own in the recess of sleep. My fear must have come from some strange nightmare I no longer could remember. I convinced myself this was the case. "You are too old to be acting like this," I heard myself say aloud as if someone was there to hear me. Of course I was trying to calm myself and to strengthen myself against whatever I was experiencing. I laughed at my own childishness. I sighed aloud due my own fear. I lay back down on my bed. I covered myself with my cover clear up to my jaw. I looked around for a third time and decided that it had been a nightmare and fitfully tried to go back to sleep. The monsters appeared to once again be just shadows, though my frightful state lingered, but was not nearly as acute.

I was not sure how long it took me to go back to sleep. But the morning was coming again as it always had. The sun would soon shine through my window and act like an alarm clock calling me from my sleep. There was a certain tranquility and peace from that fact. As it had for all my life and the lives of those before me the sun replaced the darkness of the night. Another one of the cycles in a person's life that gave to that person contentment and security in one's mortality. The storm's lightning would soon move someplace else farther from me. Perhaps to disturb another person. To instill another fear.

I was still in my cover's cocoon. It did not seem that I had moved a solitary inch from the early night's adventure of my nightmare. In my cocoon, I shivered, but I felt a sense of strength to overwhelm my sense of fear.

A fleeting thought crossed my mind, "What if it had not been a nightmare?" I chuckled at my silliness and threw back the cover. "It was just a storm. Just a silly old storm," I finally convinced myself. It was time for a new day. I bounded from my bed and look about the drabness of my room. My chair was still there. My wardrobe where my clothes were hung was awaiting me in my preparation of the new day. I threw the cover over my bed. It was not a very exact job. I had never understood why a cover had to be arranged meticulously with geometric precision and without any wrinkle or crumple smooth atop a bed. It had to be in such a manner when in just a very few hours a tired young man after a trying and hard day would wrinkle and crumple to his heart's content when he went to bed. I thought back to the many talks and discussions I had with my mother over this very topic. I had always lost the argument, but I never understood the insistence of my mom.

My morning chores of dressing and washing and readying for the day were before me. The day was coming and the sun soon would be rising. I reminded myself that I could not be tardy for Dr. Alton was to pick me up and we were to have breakfast together in the small town in which we lived.[1] I turned to leave my bedroom to begin my morning which came very, very early today.

My old bedroom door that was my barrier to the outside world and also from it was there closed before me. The door seemed a bit of a gate to a fortress and provided a sense of solitude for me, though I lived alone. Projecting from the inside of door were pegs that usually held my robe by day and my coat or some other garment by night. I grasped the door knob and felt a weirdly warm feeling. A tingle I suppose one would say. I turned and opened the door. Instantly, I was encased and enveloped by a bright and blinding light. I raised my hands to cover my eyes in a reaction due the brightness. I felt my mouth open to scream and holler. No sound ventured from my lips or throat. I saw no sight or image there for me to witness. I did not and could not see down and through the hallway that led from my bedroom to the remainder of my house. I could not see or call to anyone. That is if anyone were in my house to see or call to enable me to receive any sort of rescue.

---

[1] Dr. Alton Loveless: Publisher, Writer, Minister in the Free-Will Baptist Denomination.

----------A Different Place ----------

In a second or less of time, which seemed an eternity to me, the brightness was removed and gone from me. I was not in the door jamb. I was neither in my bedroom nor the hallway that led to my living room of my home. The light had actually been a portal and had thrown me to a new place. It was not exactly new, but a different place would be more accurate I believe. I was outside of my house and it seemed I was somewhere I had not been before, though in my own yard. The old yard had receded and a new sort of sod lay there. I looked behind me hoping my house would still be behind me. It was of course, but it seemed altered to me and my senses. "Why would I think that," I heard myself say echoing a growing portion of my internal fears and desires? The house, my house was the same color, but the colors were more intense and clear. My well of comfort and compatibility was no longer there as it once was. I had no rational explanation. I knew nothing or experience which would calm my mind or make more serene my soul. I breathed a breath and then another trying to calm my state. My legs felt like they had become rubber and I teetered a bit this and that way. I breathed another deeper breath and steadied myself and my nerve. I looked about with tentative looks. I smelled my world about me with sniffs or snorts as a horse or dog might do to explore a new place. There was a crispness and tingle in the air.

My strange place befitted the strangeness I felt. I did not feel myself. I thought to myself, "Of course silly." But it was different than just the fear of the strange and eerie that now appeared to be a constant companion since last night's storm. It was a realization that for some strange and eerie reason I felt different. I felt younger. I had no mirror, but I knew that I was no longer a young man, but a younger man. What strangeness had befallen me?

I saw about me a country side away from my house and just over the hill that led to a grove of trees. The hues of this land were of a certain color and intensity that made my previous times and experiences pale by a certain degree. I thought it most odd that like my house this new day was also intensified to my senses. The greens were greener. The browns, the blues were all greater to my eye. All the colors of the rainbow seemed more vibrant. Everything seemed more vibrant. I could not explain the difference. My words and emotions were all reeling from this new day. "What has happened to me," I thought and pondered to myself?

What sort of place where not just the colors, but the feels and the smells and the air and just everything seemed a bit above and different than the world I knew just seconds before.

I looked all around and saw the country side, but I saw no houses or barns or silos or animals or anything that I might have assumed to be in this sort of pastoral place as they once were in my before time. There was only my house. The time I remembered as before the light. They all had been there yesterday. It was as if I was by myself and alone.

There was before and behind me a winding dirt road I had travelled on so many times. That had been before the storm and the light and now it was a small road leading from behind to my front and going on to who knows where. Before the light, it had led to the small town near where I lived. It just meandered with a twist here and there. I gasped a breath. I exhaled a sigh.

I knew I must step from the lea unto the road and start a journey. No one was there who told me this. I just felt it inside. I did not know what sort of insanity or happening had just occurred to me, but it was happening to me. My tentativeness of nature had to be placed on the back burner in lieu of my present experience. I knew I could not stay where I was. I looked behind and before me, up and down the road. Being a bit of an optimist, I chose the road away from my back and before me. I started off in the direction where my town once was located.

I felt the earthen ground of the land crunch under my shoes with each step. I looked about trying to see something that would allow me to gather myself and give myself some sort of bearing in my course. I saw no animal life from the lowest to the highest animal. No birds. Not even some old crows above and about this land. It appeared it was just me and the plants and the blue sky with fluffy clouds moving above. There were trees before me on both sides of the road. I walked down the path.

After what seemed to be hours, but who could really tell a time thing without a time thing to remind a person of the time, I saw the land rising up a grade to a small hill before me. I started up the grade and with a certain exertion I topped the hill. I was standing on the lane that bore my steps since the beginning of my journey. Once again I could but gasp and breathe a deep breath from my most recent exertion. This feeling was partly from my travail and partly from my view which was now before my eyes. I had reached the end of the lane. The road had suddenly stopped and went no further and I stood at its edge. I looked over and at the other side of the hill. A massive and huge forest of trees lay before me. On past the forest, there arose another hill going farther and higher away from me. I had heard and read of the road that led to nowhere, but I thought it but a metaphor or a fanciful imaginative story. I felt as a stranger would and as a stranger could only do, I looked about me and gazed upon the immensity of the forest. I knew intrinsically it was a forest of a different sort. Since I had seen the light from my bedroom door, I was seeing many things of a different sort. I did not feel adventuresome in my daring and brave as in the days before when in my fantasy of youth it would have been allowed. I knew a fear again. I was scared of the difference.

I thought that I might turn around and go back the other way down the lane from where I had just traveled. I thought of going back to where my house was, though it was a tad different than it had been the morning before, but I talked myself out of this decision. Once you have begun a journey and find out you are travelling in a wrong direction it would seem best to stop and go the other way round and not continue down a wrong path. I had read that thought, that point of view written by a writer that I had cherished in my past. The thought of the long journey back made me more tired than I would have supposed. Perhaps that is the reason why one is reticent to turn back when one is going in the wrong direction. The thought of one's wasted effort makes one even more tired and timid. Due to the trek already endured, I convinced myself to go on farther and I decided to continue my journey. I thought to myself that perhaps I could pick up the lane somewhere in the woods if I travelled more. A type of self-rationalization I assumed. Somewhere among the trees could again lay my path. I decided to explore a bit farther into the woods and not to give up yet on my trek.

I took my first step over the crest of the hill unto the green grass and the start of the downward trek. The grass felt both lush and crunchy to my step. It was the shade of the full blown green hue of summer grass when grass was all about the growing and has yet to meet a late frost.

I began to notice the trees about and around as I looked around. They were nondescript, but something appeared odd to my eye. This oddness was more a feeling than an actual certainty I felt, but I could not be sure of anything. This tree or that tree did seem a bit out of proportion. None of the trees appeared as they would have before the light. I was in a new perception. It seemed to me a new reality. Well, as real as possible I told myself. The ones I passed grew with too many limbs on the one side and not enough on the other. Some of the trees had grown too narrow of a trunk in relation to the limbs on the top. Some leaned to the right or the left of its center with no care for balance or symmetry. I noticed some of the trees had too little or too many roots or just one root for such large trees. They precariously teetered this or that way against any gust or blow of wind. Some had too many trunks for a tree and looked a bit like stilted houses from certain foreign lands. A bit of a tree house effect I told myself. The whole of the forest just had trees that were discombobulated and cockeyed to my eye. I could make out enough to know that it was a different sort of tree in a different sort of land. This forest was numbered with a great number of trees and they lay before me. I was in the forest now and I decided to go and walk on nearer and closer toward the trees. With each step, the photograph of my vision cleared a bit more. With the clarity that comes from the nearing, the oddness of the shapes and forms of the trees seemed to grow even more oddly.

Thorny thickets grew here and there, but it was the trees which held my fancy and imagination. The thickets did grow in a hodgepodge encumbering my way as I walked toward the trees. My path, with each step, became more and more impeded. Most of the trees around seemed to be of a general sort. Just a bit strange, but I knew they were trees. Just a bit askew and they were none too straight from the ground. Though odd they were nothing much to intrigue a lad's curiosity. They were just out of kilter and different from the ideal of a tree I had in my mind or the trees before the light in my room that followed the storm. I guess that could be said for all trees, but they were still disconcerting to me. I passed several of them by and continued deeper into the forest. I continued to push my way through the bramble and bush and came close by a particular tree.

----------The Odd Rooted Tree----------

The tree was catching and a little fantastic to my eye. It was one of the trees that had drawn my gaze from afar, but now being closer, it really was something to look at. It grew from the ground, but had only one root to anchor itself into the ground. The root grew up and within from the ground; twisting about trying to secure the tree to its soil. Any person could see something was amiss. The trunk became gnarly and knotted and rough-barked due to not being well nourished and only anchored by having the solitary root. There was only one limb that grew from the oddly shaped trunk. It was quite a sight. From the solitary limb grew only leaves with only one or two fruit at the end of the limb. The fruit was oddly shaped and looked a bit malformed. "This was an uncommon tree in the midst of trees akin in uncommonness," I muttered aloud to myself. I thought to myself how truly peculiar this tree was in fact. When one gets closer to a source how more clearly one can see.

"Now that is a tree that is incredibly weird." The voice came from behind and I spun toward the sound. There stood a man. A reasonably tall man when compared to my idea of the normal. Of course to a lad all grownups are tall. In my predicament and place, I was coming to think as a younger lad in lieu of what I had been before the storm and the light. I gazed and looked over toward the origin of the voice trying to get the gist of the man. He was dressed in a suit coat and tie. He was wearing a vest. For all his suit and vest, he was crumpled and looked as if he had had a long day in the forest. He held a pipe in his one hand and wiped his forehead of sweat with a handkerchief with the other. His stance and his demeanor exuded a studious and learned appearance. "I have seen many a tree in my day, but that is all out of sorts. Don't you think?" I was taken aback by his talk. I had not seen him approach me until I turned around hearing his voice. I took a step or two backing away from him. He smiled a dry intelligent wry smile and nodded as if he seemed to understand my situation. The man placed his handkerchief back into his side coat pocket and held out his right hand upward in a sign of peace as if to reassure me that all was well. I could not help but think it was strange that he put the kerchief into the right side pocket instead of his back trouser pocket. I guess he wanted to keep it at the ready for use to mop at his forehead if the occasion arose. I could but mumble out a few words. They were not even words really in reply to the man. More like a, "hmmm," or an, "uhhh," but I finally managed to get out a, "Where did you come from," with the greatest of effort? Folks when startled are not incredibly articulate are they?

He just chuckled a bit and hitched his coat to a more comfortable position on his shoulders and pulled up his britches. He almost appeared to be readying for his own journey. His face a bit haggard and lined with age and experience spoke to me of an intelligence and wisdom. His hair was thinning and parted in an absent-minded sort of way. The man was none the worried at my failure to ask anything but the obvious. He chuckled again and looked at me with a smile and said to me, "I love the trees. Even these weirdly shaped ones in this part of the forest. They try so very hard, but have just missed the mark a bit. Don't you think?"

I noticed that his speech was different than my Midwestern American draw. It was very English or Irish or something from over in that part of the world. Not that I had ever been there. I had barely been out of my local county, but I had heard that accent on the television. "You are not from around here are you?" He chuckled with a hearty and hale chuckle that made a person feel at ease quickly and completely. "No I am not, but I have been in this forest for many a day and night. I have made it my study now in this place of my life. This forest you see. I have never seen a forest exactly such as this. I look at this tree and that tree and try to glimmer and glean some knowledge and understanding. Do you like this tree," asked the gentleman? "It seems strange to my eye," I responded. The man walked up to the tree and patted its gnarly knotted bark with a pat that a person might give a relative who had given you some reason to be exasperated and perplexed. He exhaled a sigh and turned to me and said, "I am a bit worn out by my travels today. Let's find a spot on that luscious grass away from these ever present thickets and barbs and briars and sit a bit. That is if you don't mind?" As he spoke, he pointed in a direction away from this tree we were discussing. I looked at this suited man in a crumpled suit and felt at ease. He seemed to be a day to day sort of person despite his suit. He came across as a common sort, but with a quick wit. I watched him turn from the gnarled tree and started to walk away from it. Pushing back a bit of the brambling thicket, he made a trail away from the tree. I cleared my throat with another, "hmmmm," and started to follow him. "I would like that," I heard myself say. "You are not from around here are you?"

The thicket that grew close to the tree played out in a bit and there was the grassy area that seemed inviting to the man. He eyed the spot with a keen eye and in a most spry manner sat and sprawled out a bit on the green and lush grass. I heard the crunch of the grass. He sat down in such a relaxing manner it was as if he were readying himself for a picnic of a sort. He made a sweeping motion with his arm in invitation to me. I soon found myself standing close by this man. "It would seem proper for an introduction," replied my new acquaintance. "I have a very long and proper name, but you may call me Jack."[2] "You do not seem like a Jack to me," I replied. But with a quick look and a smile he informed me that a long time before he had chosen Jack as his name. I remember he said in a matter of fact manner, "Jack is a good name. A day to day name and that is the name I have chosen and Jack it is!" I agreed with him and told him that Jack was a good name and that I had only meant that in his suit though crumbled I thought he would have a more grown up and fancy name. I quickly apologized for the mention of the wrinkles and crumbles. I felt like I might have insulted him. With him being the only person who I had seen in the forest, I was not ready or willing to alienate him. He quickly reassured me with a raise of his hand as if to stop me in my attempt of apology. "I have always seemed to be crumply in my clothes. To many, I appear a plumber or butcher or some other sort." I interrupted again trying to complete my apology, but he continued, "Oh, I do not care about the occasional wrinkle or crumple. I tend to forget my pipe being lit and my, oh, the holes I have burnt into my jacket." I interrupted him again and said, "You seem to be an intelligent sort of person. You might be the person who might help me explain my

---

[2] Professor Clive Staples Lewis: Literary Professor at Oxford and Cambridge, Writer, Poet, Theologian, and Philosopher.

situation?" "Oh," replied Jack. "You have a situation?" "My yes, I really do, sir." I spent the next several minutes telling Jack of the last night and the storm and the light at the door jamb and the journey up to this point of time. For some reason, I felt comfortable with him, both in conversation and proximity. I even shared with him I had a fear about my lot which I now found myself.

Jack took it all in. He rubbed his cheek and stroked his hair. He mulled things over before he spoke. He was that sort of fellow. "It appears to me," Jack replied in a thoughtful manner, "That something strange has happened to you to bring you here to this forest of trees. I would have supposed that it would take a storm and something magical and strange for you to find yourself here. Do not let the storm or the light concern you. I should think that it is the trees and this woodland that should gather and keep your attention in the here and now. I know a bit about this forest. I know something about that tree you were gazing upon a moment ago. I study and ponder on such things as my hobby. But there is one thing for sure that I do not know my good lad. What would happen to be your name? You have me at a great disadvantage my good Sir!" I laughed a bit more from the additional embarrassment of another slip of my manners than anything clever or funny or humorous. "I am so sorry Jack. I do not know what is wrong with me. My name is David. David Longing," I further amplified. "Ah, David pull up a chair." He once again swept his arm around the glen as if he was directing me to a chair or a sofa in a warm and inviting den or sitting room. I found an inviting patch of grass and sat close near Jack.

"Ah," continued Jack, "you were pondering that unusual tree back where we first met I believe?" "Yes sir," I replied. "It seemed most unusual to me. All out of sorts and lop sided." "That is not unusual David. You will find my good lad that in this wood a good many trees may seem out of sorts as you say." Many are not even in the big game so to speak. Some are in the game, but are just out from the ideal norm. He looked away a bit toward and around where he sat. He breathed several breaths rapidly and more heavily as if a weighty burden sat on his chest. He looked at me soon enough and gave a comforting and wry smile. "This tree like most trees grows to its advantage and nurture. A tree will grow out of proportion if it leans a certain way. It will grow a certain way. I have a reason for being here at this time with you David. I have come to introduce you to this forest. For some reason, you are here and from here you must travel. Go my lad through this wood and you will find the most remarkable things to view." "I don't know what you mean," I added quickly. "Of course not David how could you? One must experience a thing, sense a thing, and consume a thing to really know a thing. If you do not know something, how could a person know something? The secret is to find out," he said as if he had said this same thing to many a person with a question due a situation. "I will give you a bit of advice. Never assume that each tree to be the same as another or to expect that the entire forest is made up of the same sort as you find here. Travel your path and your journey will be the more rich for the journey," Jack stopped for a second and breathed in a deep breath and then he went on, "Explore and experience and eat up the journey.

Too many people ignore the simple fact that to know is to experience and you can only experience by jumping in there. Always remember this fact. A person must jump in a lake so to speak to get wet. The best swimming, when wet is always in the deep water. The deep water also gives you the most danger for it is over your head, but it is still the best swimming. In shallow streams and lakes one may get a bit wet, but one cannot stretch out and float and roll about and be immersed in the water. Knowledge is the same sort of creature. To know something, you must baptize yourself in the deep water. This forest gives to you that opportunity. Consider yourself on your journey to be akin to swimming and frolicking in a lake. Experience and immerse yourself and you will find that more and more you will know and understand your journey in the forest. I hope I am not confusing or mixing my metaphors, but please understand me. You will find many sorts and ilks of trees, but the task is to see the trees. Even those trees that are not the normal can allow a person to glean the ideal from the tree's lack of a this or a that. Do not ignore them as you walk through this forest. Literally do not miss the trees for the forest," he chuckled again at his paradox of a most common saying. "Jump into the water so to speak and enjoy the swim." I liked Jack from the start. One must surely like this person with a quick wit and a quick laugh. To see the humor of this man is a wonderful experience, I thought to myself.

I found myself captivated by Jack's talk. I caught myself sitting in this clearing and leaning forward with my head resting upon one of my hands propped up as one might find any school boy or girl listening to a story by the library lady at my local library. I was enraptured by the telling of the tale. I was in awe of the words, the elegant words that Jack had said. I did not know much, but I was here and the forest lay before me. Jack knew that I was captured by the thought. "Wisdom and intelligence expressed with simplicity," I thought to myself. He smiled, but not in a smug way, but in a way of a fellow traveler. "But Jack, how will I know about this tree. It was discombobulated and askew. It must have in its nature concentrated on its one root or its leaves and not on its whole nature." "Ah yes," replied Jack, "I see you are the right sort for this sort of trip. The journey has only started and you are already asking good questions. Now is more of a time to observe the differences. Answers may come later. Look and see and enjoy and I will be about, here and there and we can talk. You trip is but starting. Look for the knowledge and the understanding will be its byproduct my good lad," he said ending the sentence with a gusto and vigor raising a clenched fist upward in a sort of punch in the air! "Remember it is the trip that leads to a conclusion and not the solitary moment during the trip."

"You must go through the forest for it seems all must and it is your time now," continued Jack in his speech. "Too many, yes too many stop here and there with a particular tree and get caught up in its form. You must remember when one is at the end of the journey comes the enlightenment of greater knowledge more so than just the one experience. In the end, it will be the time for you to draw a conclusion and come to an answer. It will be your time." He rubbed his chin and reached for his pipe he carried in his pocket. He thumped the pipe's bowl and replaced the old tobacco with new and began his smoke. I watched the bluish smoke rise from the bowl and float above his head heading upward into the sky. I saw the twinkle in his eye. He was in peace with himself. He seemed to enjoy his task of explaining to one as ignorant as I. I knew I was enjoying myself. Enjoying a moment which was such a change from the earlier dread I had felt at the start of my trip. My talk with Jack had encouraged and strengthened me to such a greater degree.

Time, to my mind, came and went as the two of us just sat there and enjoyed the moment. Time passed differently. Time was secondary in importance. The meeting and the time together was the important thing. In a bit, Jack cleared his throat with a loud, "Grrrrufff," and he tapped the pipe's bowl on the knee of his trousers and emptied the now dead tobacco and placed the empty, but still warm pipe in his coat pocket. "You must be on your way and I have things to do," he said to me with both a quizzical and thoughtful manner as he stood from the comfort of his sitting place on the clearing. I took my cue from him and stood to my feet. I faced Jack and said, "Go where," and I continued, "I have no idea where I am going?" Jack replied, "I thought I have made that obvious and clear David. You must go through the forest, through the trees. It is necessary for you to go on this trek." "Necessary for whom," I answered? "Well, necessary for you that is for sure and for me and for the forest. For everything, I should say. One person's trek and travail always affects all things around him and much farther than just the close, but also the whole. It is somewhat like that butterfly scenario thing that people are always speaking." "Are you sure," I answered my new friend, somewhat befuddled and trying to grasp his meaning? The manner of his speech spoke volumes that I would soon be alone again in this forest. I did not look forward to being alone. "Are you sure," I repeated myself? "My, yes for I must go, but remember I will be around; here and there, as needed. I have so enjoyed our brief chat. Travel well David Longing. Travel far and see the forest.

Enjoy the deeper water of your swim," he said with a smile and a wink.

Both of us stood there for several additional seconds of time. Not saying anything. We just were looking at each other. With a sigh, I turned away from my new friend. I faced toward the forest and continued my walk. Through the clearing, I soon came back into the bramble of the thickets. I thought to myself how soon and quickly over was this interval of rest for a lad. How too soon over was the contentment of my time with Jack. I turned back in the direction I once had been and Jack stood there looking at me. He waved his upward hand while holding the pipe which was once again removed from his jacket pocket. He soon turned and walked away from me in another direction with a purposeful and striding gait. A gait that demonstrated a walk much practiced and experienced. I turned back to my thicket and my chore. I did not feel very purposeful. I just felt alone. With Jack in my mind and thoughts, I turned away from his ever diminishing figure and back to the future of my journey.

------------MORE ODD TREES------------

I continued my progression bursting through one thicket only to find more and more of the brambly shrubs. I found myself worried they would never end. Perhaps that is the way of the trek, I found myself sidetracking in my thoughts. One is looking for one thing or a particular thought only to find there is always an impediment and a hindrance. It was a type of a mental and physical chore which proved to be an impeding hindering wall making my progress harder and more arduous as a seeker. I pushed and attacked and was in turn pushed back and attacked by the thorny sticks fighting my advance. The continuing pestering of these brambles became a sort of gnat or gadfly to me. It seemed like so many hours, but finally, I made my way through the traps of nature and came upon another clearing. I heaved and panted trying to restore my breath to a normal rate. I looked about me to gather in my new lot. I did not see as many of the shrubs, but there was a stand of trees. There were short trees and tall trees. There were old trees thick and rigid about the middle with age and time. There were young trees still agile and supple moving about without the rigidity that comes due to time and age.

They all had one thing in common. They were all shaped, both young and old; somewhat like the tree I had seen when I first met Jack. They all suffered from the same condition. They grew from the ground with only one root. The limbs and trunks did not trouble me as I zeroed in on the one root. At this moment, I felt overwhelmed by the oddness and unusualness of this matter. These trees were a type of community which held to a common trait. They appeared to be less anchored into the soil by the single root than the trees of my previous experiences. The trees of course which were before the storm and the light. I pondered in this almost wishful moment of my past memory and then continued my observation. I looked at both the old ones and the young ones. They had just the one root. The trunk grew out of proportion to the root. It twisted a bit and the trunks of the trees could not and did not grow straight upward as would a normal tree.

I found myself laughing at that thought. Not at the condition of the trees, but that I would bring into play what I thought was normal. "Not here," I found myself saying out loud. "Not here. What was normal a bit ago could not be held to these trees. I am in a different sort of woods now,"I thought to myself. "How in the world can these trees stand for so long?" Anyone could see the peril of this forest. Any old wind could come and blow anyone of these trees down. I looked about and that is exactly what I saw. Scattered through the forest, upturned and fallen trees lay about dead. The single root did not allow and afford these trees any anchoring or security. The fallen trees were just rotting in decay. "No support. No support at all," I said out loud again to no one, but myself and stating the obvious.

"So many trees aground and dead," I thought to myself. "They once were alive, but for some reason their roots never grew properly." A tree, to be a healthy tree, must be rooted to withstand the winds that may blow. The roots must be proper in order for the tree trunk and the limbs to receive water and food from the earth.

The trees that were standing were sickly and malignant and warped. Whether tall or short, they all made for a curious sight indeed. The root came out and hitched around like a crooked big toe of an older person or something akin to that. The trunk, askew and bent grew out from the crooked root trying to reach for the skies above, but always trying to fight the handicap of the single root. Each tree appeared to be at a disadvantage from the start due its retardation.

I was pondering the shape and scope of the trees in this little wood. They all suffered from the same condition. I was lost in my thoughts and was startled from a voice behind me. It was not an eerie memory of a recent past moment like my meeting Jack. It was a voice so familiar, but so long removed from my hearing. "Hello son, it's me, your Dad."[3] I spun around. Whether due the spinning or the shock of hearing my father's voice I do not know, but I was rocked and reeled by the moment. I thought I was going to faint. "Dad," was all I could say. I found myself reaching for some support, but found none. The older man reached and grabbed me before I fell to the ground. His strength and support held me up for the time I needed to regain a bit of composure. "Dad, Dad," I repeated with an even higher voice. "Yes son, it is me. I thought I would come for a bit and help you through this forest. I have missed you David." I felt a tear welling up in my eyes and in my heart seeing once again his face of wisdom and age. "You must have a million questions or more I would imagine. Remember this is a different sort of place. Time is different here." I gasped a heavy sigh and looked at my Father. "How is this possible," I asked myself in my mind? It was he. I knew it was my Dad. My Dad who had been absent and apart so long from me. I, since that day, that terrible day, had carried a hole in my heart and a longing thought in my mind about him. I could

---

[3] Mr. Charles Kenith Clarke.

only stare in a disbelief I guess he could see. It was written on my face. "Let's go over here and sit on that big log on the ground." I heard him say. With me in tow, Dad and I walked the short distance to the fallen log and sat down.

I still could only gaze at my Dad. I could not yet speak. His hand that held my shoulder in support was his in every way, but they didn't seem as old and feeble as the last time I had seen them. I turned my head almost with a fear to look upon his face. I saw his hair and his features. I saw his eyes and the smile on his lips. His look bespoke of a cleverness which always seemed ready to spring like a wild cat with a quip or a comment on some unwary prey. I had missed this face which for all my life had been the world to me. I had missed it too long. It is not that he looked young, for he looked old, but he looked healthy and complete. I still remembered the parting days when he left me. He had been so frail at last and then gone. I thought to myself, "Is this a dream? How is this possible?" Dad patted me on the shoulder as he released me from his grasp. "I know son. It is so inexplicable, but this is a different sort of forest. I have come to help you through its maze and perhaps we can talk a bit. I have missed you, but I have not been gone from you as you might have supposed. In this timberland, one finds a world in symbol and sight not of time and supposed reality as in the other place. These trees are not only true, but are what happened and what may have happened in our experiences.

I have been sent and asked to help you along the way." I looked at his face again. If this be a hallucination or a specter or a ghost I could not say, but "No," I thought to myself and then said it aloud with a questioning voice. "No?" "I know it is hard to get a handle on," I heard him say.

I knew that it was he for the hole in my heart that had been a constant and non-stopping pain was now gone and healed. With the pain's departure, my total being told me it was Dad. I smiled at him; not understanding, but welcoming him. I found myself quiet which was unusual for me.

Before now and back then, before that day, Dad and I could talk about all sorts of things. The things I learned from him in conversation and company I held precious. When he had gone from me, they were more valuable in my memory than any inheritance of any property or money. "Dad," taking a deep breath to steel and bolster my nerve, "How is this?" I found myself resting my hand on his shoulder as I repeated my question, "How is this possible? Is this real? You, how is this," not fully finishing my question? I guess part of me in my ignorance was somewhat afraid of the answer. Dad laughed that chuckle of his. I had heard it for all my life. I knew it clear and what it was for it had been engrained within my heart and etched upon my brain. He smiled, during his laugh, that smile that had been a centering focus to me for so many of my years. He had been the North Star to me and had guided me during much of my journey and now he was back. However this miracle or why ever this appearance of Dad, I no longer cared. It was Dad. I felt, well, I just felt. Contentment, joy, I did not possess nor could I grasp nor was it possible to own the right words, but I just felt fine. I felt just fine with him once again.

I took in his appearance, his face and his build. Everything about Dad while not younger was complete in its nature and appearance. No pain or want or lack was evident in anything about him. He was still wearing the blue work shirt he had liked and always seemed to wear for as long as I could remember. His blue work pants spoke of a man who had labored long and hard in his life. Those twinkling eyes were behind glasses long familiar to me. He reached with his right hand and adjusted his glasses upon his face as he had done incalculable times. He not only looked like Dad, but his being was Dad, both healthy and here.

"You must have a score of questions for me, but they will have to wait a bit. I have come to talk about these trees you have found yourself among in this forest. Do they seem oddly shaped to you?" "Well yes," I replied. "I was just pondering on that very thing when you came to me." Dad chuckled once again and said, "Yes son I could have guessed that you were. I like the word 'ponder'. That is why I chuckled just now. The world you live in doesn't ponder enough does it," asked my Dad?

My father had always been a philosopher. Not in an academic sense, but in a practical sense. He was a conversational philosopher. He had always been an observer of his time and being. Remembering my recent new friend Jack, had he not written that it was never a question of philosophy or no philosophy, but a question of good philosophy or bad philosophy? I remembered and I knew now who Jack was. It had come to me. He was a writer. He was a famous writer of books. He had penned many of the very books that I had loved to read over the years. He was one of my favorite writers and there he was just recently standing before me. First Jack and now my father had come to me in this forest.

Perhaps, it now occurred to me that I had died in the light. This very thought was my passing thought at this moment. Perhaps, it was true that when one passed over into the eternal they saw a great light. I had heard such talk from folk who had said they had died and crossed over to the other side. I spoke like dying was akin to crossing a creek or river. I guess in some ways it was. One found oneself on one side of a river's shore line for only a bit of time. Then one was on the other shore. What did the Good Book call the change: "A twinkling of an eye?" Perhaps it was that quick. I did not know for sure whether I had died or not, but I did for sure see a great white light. The change had happened in a quick speck of time. Seeing Jack and now my father made my head reel. I began to rock on the log where Dad and I were sitting. My arm fell down from my father and I found myself hugging myself in some effort to comfort and control myself. Dad rested his hand on my shoulder as he had in so many ways and times prior to now. It was as if he was trying to steady me. I felt so overwhelmed. But as it had for all those years and times, that strong hand did comfort and steady me.

"Try son not so much to understand this time, this forest or this place, but feel and see and observe it. Understanding things like one did before the light is not the same sort of operation as now. I know about the light. Before the light, one could only sense and know in a limited fashion. Your being was but a partial understanding. Now is not so much a time for understanding in a conventional sense, but to understand it in a complete sense. You see son here belief and seeing and knowing and understanding is a one thing and not a varied incomplete thing. To understand 'is' as He 'is'. I turned to Dad and said, "Dad I don't understand in any sense." Dad laughed out a reply, "Of course not son. That is why I am here. I feel that you have already sensed and felt and observed something is off concerning these trees, right?" "Well, yes," I replied. "I was asking myself about that very matter when you came as to how it would be possible for these trees to stand for very long. In fact, I just saw all those many trees that had fallen and lay rotting and dead due the fact that they could not brave and last the winds that blew against them." Dad's eyebrows raised and his eyes grew bright behind his glasses with an added twinkle as he said, "That is right son. How near you are. If you only knew how near you are.

These trees have one root, but you have also seen trees with two or more roots. Trees with multiple trunks or with just a limb or two, but in this stand you see a stand of a particular type of tree. These are the trees of only one root. Roots give to the tree in its entirety, sustenance and water from the ground. From the soil of the earth, the roots give to the tree. A proper tree in this forest needs two roots to anchor itself into the ground. One root is for the hearing and the other for encouragement. No tree can be healthy and sustain itself from the winds of existence with only the one and without the other. It would only be partially anchored.

The One who made the forest and is from beyond the forest has made in His perfection a way and a plan for each of His trees. The One above all the forests and above you and me has decided and decreed that all trees should have the two roots. One of the Word and one of the Spirit. Of course, I am speaking of a perfect tree, a tree in His ideal. Apart from His ideal, any other tree is askew and imperfect. He has sent me to you at this time to help you as you go through this forest. Perhaps, you may have some questions for me. I will try to answer them. Remember I am your Dad, but I am just me. I will try to help you. You see David as you might have already guessed we are not talking about trees. We are talking of human folk. We are talking of you and me."

I grasped my head with both of my hands. So much made no sense to me. From the difference of this forest, the storm, and the light still left me muddled and addled in my brain. So much made sense before, but this was now and I was in a different place. I was seeing people who had been gone, but who were now here. Here and now in this particular forest. I had seen many trees back in my other time. None had roots like these about me now. Many had differing and odd numbered and shaped roots. The tree of His ideal has two roots. All others are not of His ideal. But these trees stood out in both mind and sense. The normal of this place could not be compared to the normal of my before place. "This was a different sort of place," I reminded myself. Even due my fog of brain, I was gleaning that this was a forest of the symbol and the metaphor. I could barely maintain in my previous life the fantasy of reality, but now I found myself in the reality of the fantasy.

Dad reached over again and this time with both hands grasped both of my hands in his firm grip. "I know, I know," was all he said. He stood while still holding my hands forcing me and urging me to also stand. "I know," was all he said in that moment. He began to walk about the clearing among the log we had been sitting upon and the other trees both standing and fallen. Dad continued his talking about this ilk of a tree. "If a person holds too strong and ignores one root over another it becomes warped. Like this tree or that one," he stretched out his arm and with his hand extending his pointing finger; he pointed in a panorama of the trees about us. He pointed at old trees which clearly had used but the one root for so long that the root dwarfed any potential and had grown like the old man toes and looped over parts of the trunk. The root of knowing or the other trunk of feeling had retarded the tree and even, when carried to the extreme had bent the trunk this or that way. The tree still attempted to grow and flourish, but at a disability and disadvantage from the way it should be growing. With both of the roots, the tree would grow straight and tall and nourished. Winds always blow and these partially rooted trees were less able to stand the blow, but with the two roots as prescribed by the One, a tree can stand the test.

"But Dad I now understand. Well I think I understand a bit more about the tree's roots and the twoness necessary for this forest. This forest is as it was meant to be by the One. But Dad you have said that one root is for learning and knowing and the other is for feeling in an experiential way. What about all of that," I asked him in a manner which even to me seemed to present a bit of urgency?"

"David," as my father began to answer me. "To know is to learn. The one root is His word. The Son has communicated the word. The Son spoke the word. His word was the word of God for He is God the Son. We must know and learn it. Whatever a person puts into their mind rests in their being, their heart as some have said and written before in other books. A picture fills the vision of the eyes. A tune fills the hearing of the ears. A good meal, a good drink fills the taste of the stomach. The word fills the longing of the soul and heart of a person. The Son has spoken certain things that have been written down for all of us. We as believers are to learn from the word and practice it. The word of God is a living word. It is truly an immutable and progressive word. As God never changes nor does His word, but it has been progressively revealed. As one begins at the beginning God has revealed certain promises to certain people, but as the reader continues, these promises have been altered and more progressively demonstrated by the One. Always due to the continual disobedience and disbelief of the reader, the word is then open to be further revealed and enhanced by the speaker of the word, the One. If a person took the time to read the word as he would read any other book, he would see that it is written in a context. Remember Son," I heard my Dad's voice rise a bit in emphasis and he continued clapping one hand upon the other in an additional emphasis as a conductor might to keep time in a musical score. Each word or phrase received a clap. "A text taken out of context is only a pretext! Any book taken out of context can be made to say all manner of things. The worst of all things is to present a thought, but only partially. Some man in a day gone by once said that the most effective lie is one that is ninety nine percent true. To take something from its context to prove or should I say misprove a particular point is to offer only the pretext of a lie. It is worse when we are dealing with the word of the One. He is truth and not partial truth. He is knowledge and not a partial knowledge. His word, His scripture is total and not just the trite and partial offerings of explanations of would be sages and teachers. Inevitably when a reader skews and perverts a text into a pretext it cannot help but warp the root of knowledge and learning for a tree, for a particular person. This one root must be true to the truth. It must be in line with the Truth Giver. To ignore the Truth Giver and His true word cannot help but retard the growth of a particular tree in this forest. This fact is true for any tree. The word acts as a root for the tree and provides nourishment and education. It buffers the tree against the storms and winds of delusion and distraction and the antiwords from antigod individuals and causes.

The weight of his words hit upon my brain as a hammer might pound upon an anvil in some blacksmith shop. His words of instruction were like driving metal upon metal under an intense heat in the chore of pounding a third thing or item into a useful tool for some worker or person. The truth of Dad's words hit me hard and I knew he was speaking the truth. To learn and know a new something in a more complete manner was like that tool being straightened and shaped by the smith with a hammer and anvil. The process can be a forceful and hard act. It was so for me. A thousand thoughts made me grimace and twitch as that third thing with each blow. Truth is truth and speaks of a Truth Giver. No amount of relativistic sophistry or false wisdom could or can alter that fact. I thought back of the time when I would and did hear of a speaker say this or that, but in the light of a total truth it was only a boiled and rendered down partial thought. Half of a something is still but a half of nothing. I look toward my father and he was still there. He had turned to another tree and he started to speak once again.

"But there are two roots to be considered. "The one is for knowing and learning while the second is for experiencing and feeling. The second root is a necessary root, but it is a complementary root of the first. This root is the Spirit. It is spiritual and like the breath of God it instills into each tree, each trunk the evidence of the reality of the tree. It demonstrates the ownership of the tree. David we are talking of the God of the universe and if a tree is to be His it must be guided by Him. He has determined that the root of knowing, Scripture, will be evidenced by the root of experience and feeling, the Spirit. It is His plan and as such is the true way for any tree in any forest to grow correctly. Oh I know you are seeing different sorts of trees, but David there is only one sort of tree that is purposed to grow straight and true.

If a tree has only the root of knowing and does not demonstrate the evidence and guidance of the root of feeling and experiencing, then the tree becomes dry and warped. The tree or the person might become egotistical in self-important thinking. That sort of one dimensional tree is thereby presenting a form of knowledge and truth for the entire world to see. Not however presenting a true demonstration of the One.

On the other hand, if a tree only has the root of feeling, if might askew itself to thinking that only the experience is the necessary attribute for any particular tree. It would become self-important again, but in a different manner. The tree or a person might somehow feel it necessary to rally around the saying, 'better felt that telt.' It would grow and bend to the experiential root and demand that all other trees bend to that particular experience. Without the truth of the knowing, it would become ignorant and fall under a particular experience when given and offered as a counterfeit by others outside of the tree. Winds and storms of delusion assail against the trees without the root of knowing. Also, the winds and storms of ignorance assail and fight against the trees without the root of experience. Without the root of feeling and the root of knowing together, those same winds will attack a tree because it is ignorant being self-absorbed in a singular experience."

In another flash of light, not one like in my own bedroom, but this one just merely clarity of knowledge and understanding, I knew a more complete thing. The light was a bit like the proverbial light bulb coming on in the dark. Faith is not removed from knowledge. Knowledge is not an enemy of experience. Experience is not the antithesis of reason and knowledge and truth.

I looked at my father and I saw he had stopped talking and breathed heavily not only due to exertion, but also due the heaviness of the thoughts he had been conveying to me. I could but take in the words and thoughts and I too could but breathe in heavily. It was like breathing in a heavy air.

"So, son a tree must have both roots to anchor itself into the ground," my father continued. "Of course, you know and understand that I am speaking of human folk. The trees are a symbol of a particular sort of person. A person might hold too fast to a type of knowledge while ignoring the teacher and guide. The other is a person that seeks and grasps the feeling and ignores the word. Both roots are necessary and are ordained by the One to anchor and steady the tree into the ground of our life for the One. It is His plan and to deviate from it can only lead to what you see here in this forest of the one rooted trees. They warp and skew and finally fall and rot and decay because their anchors, in one manner or the other, where not developed and grown and present to prevent the disaster of the storm."

Dad looked around the forest of the one rooted trees and then said to me, "Come with me Son. We must go on. Your trek while long is just beginning and is not over I believe." Dad reached out and took my hand as he had done when I was a small child and began to lead me through the fallen and misshaped and one rooted trees. He led me around the bramble bushes and the thorny growths. Dad seemed to know the ways to avoid them all. Soon the one rooted trees appeared to thin a bit and the decaying and rotting fallen trees where scarce in number. Dad looked at me and said, "David remember about the roots. One must be balanced as He would have us balanced. In life, a person can always find a person or a cause, a thing here or a thing there that would say that it is not necessary or so, but son it is. True wisdom still, even in this day, comes from the One. Just because a sophist or supposed seer comes around and about does not mean he is correct. Remember the two roots of the knowing and the feeling and your tree will be rooted and will grow straight and upward towards the One." We continued walking and finally reached a small clearing and another stand of trees lay before us. I heard my Dad sigh a sigh. It seemed to me that he had reached a conclusion to his remarks and conversation with me.

"Dad there is another stand in front of us. You are going to help me on and through those also aren't you," I heard myself ask my father in a bit of a desperate tone? Dad replied to me, "No son. I have been sent to help you through a particular stand, but you have further and farther to travel. Don't worry or fret. Always keep in mind that the reality is the two rooted tree. All others are but a variation away from the perfection that He would have us. I know that soon and very soon we will see each other again. Remember time is but a mortal transition and construct. Time is not here and now, but only in your previous time. When we see each other again it will be as if we have never been apart. Do not worry. Eternity is before us all and we will spend it together with the One. It is set and determined by the One. The

Father and the Son and the Spirit has decided these things and matters. He is above time and space and even the material. He is and that is good enough for me and I know it is good enough for you. I love you Son and travel well the rest of your journey." "I love you too Dad," I replied. "Travel well!" I saw Dad point to the new stand and I looked to where he was pointing and saw the stand. I looked back to where my Dad had been and saw that he was gone. Space had given way and Dad had left me. I sighed another sigh, but I knew that this time, "Time," I said aloud. "What a word." This happening or occurrence was not final, but only a separation. I would see Dad again and it would be like we had never been apart.

----------TREES WITH TRUNKS----------

I looked at the new stand of trees that lay before me and knew my journey would continue there. I began to cross the clearing where Dad had finished his all too short walk and talk with me. The trees were before me. I saw a person sitting among several of the trees. I looked and looked again fearing my eyes were as askew as some of the trees about me. It was so strange to see him just sitting there. He was actually sitting in a chair and he was reading a book. In the middle of this forest, he could have just as well been in his den in his home. Sitting and passing the day reading his favorite book. Even from this distance one can tell he was a man with age. One could also tell he was thin, almost frail in his build and stature. He had a face wrinkled a bit with age and with a shock of white hair growing from his head. The closer I walked toward him the less old and frail he seemed to me. His oldness and frailness seemed to give way to wisdom and knowledge and experience. I thought I recognized him. Getting the more near to him bred a familiarity and closeness that made me the more willing and anxious to be near him.

I kept walking and in just a bit I was close to him. He seemed with my proximity to sense me and he looked up from his book. In a very familiar and baritone voice with his words drawled and warbling and with a slight quaver he said, "I've been waiting for you. Where have you been?" I stumbled over my words. Meeting Jack and then Father was almost too much to fathom and grasp and now to look upon this man that I remembered as Doctor and a teacher of mine nearly floored me with a sudden rush of memory.[4] "I, um, I have come right along. I was not expecting you." The man closed his book. With both hands, he reached to the arms of his chair and forced himself up from his seat. Standing from his seat, he was a bit bowed of back. At times I wanted to rush to him for he would teeter a bit this way and that way. Then in the nick of time, he would balance himself as if this readjustment was a common occurrence. The doctor repeated himself once again, "Where have you been? It seems that I have been reading my book there by these trees for such a long time. I have had such a wonderful time here in this forest reading and observing the trees." I did not how to respond to this man from my past and my memory. "I am sorry Doctor," was all I could manage to reply in such a very lame way. I had remembered in my past he was just a very wise teacher. Doctor had always been a humble and retiring sort, but with a hint of mischievousness shining from his eyes. He had the wisdom of life spent in study, but he had God's love in his heart. These two aspects together meant that he would share his time. He had shared his time with me. He took his right weathered hand and brushed his hair backwards away from his face. I stared at Doctor and saw what I had seen so many times. The man always seemed to be dressed in the nattiest of ways. His clothes were old and passé according to modern standards, but there was always a tie tied around his neck and a suit jacket always worn. There was a handkerchief always at the ready and kept in the side pocket of his jacket. I thought to myself how unusual that Doctor shared this same habit with Jack.

---

[4] Dr. Ora Lovell, Professor, Writer, and Pastor of the Churches of Christ in Christian Union.

I looked up once again and saw he was waving at me to come near him. I left my spot and walked towards him. "Well, David how have you been? It seems just the longest of time since we have spoken. On the other hand, it seems like yesterday." "Doctor I know what you mean. This is surely an odd and strange forest. I have seen the writer, Jack and that was such a joy. He explained so much to me. Then right after that I saw Dad." I turned and pointed back up the trail from which I came." I saw him right over there. I did not think it possible to see my father again. Both Jack and Dad were explaining to me about this forest and the trees. It was such an interesting conversation I had with both of them and to hear of the different trees in this forest: to discuss why in this forest the trees meant so many things. I learned of the importance of the trees having the two roots necessary for growth. I also learned that there could be trees of varying types."

The doctor seemed to become excited. He could hardly control himself. I had seen him in this way before. A passage of Scripture or the usage of a particular Greek word or phrase could create within him and to anyone near him the most wonderful of talks. "Yes, yes that is exactly why I'm here. You see David each tree has some sort of root. But as you know only trees with perfect roots are able to grow perfectly as He desires. With the Word and the Spirit anchoring, feeding and nourishing the tree, one can see amazing growth. Each tree's growth in its perfection grows into the straightest of trunks. Now David not many do grow straight. To be perfect or to be complete can be a rare thing. A very precious event it is for sure. You see I am talking about the trunk of the tree, but each tree is a symbol for each person. Many of the trees lean this way and that way and are crooked. But if the roots are anchored in the Lord's good soil, each tree can grow straight, ramrod straight towards the sun. At the risk of repeating myself or what others have said or written, remember David that the two roots stand in symbol. The trunk also stands in symbol. David this is the typical nature for these woods."

The doctor paused and drew in a deep breath. I used this pause to breathe in a very deep breath myself. I tried to understand what the doctor was telling me. I knew that this was just the beginning of his explanation. I turned my head to the right and to the left and I looked at the trees around and about both the doctor and myself. Some of the trees had the straightest of trunks. Many of the others did in fact grew aslant from the ground.

The doctor, my teacher continued, "To know how this may occur, a person must examine the trunk of the tree. For a perfect and complete tree, a finished tree will grow straight as I have said. The trunk of the tree is the strength of the tree. The trunk of the tree is the body of the tree. In much the same way, our walks with our Lord must have strength to weather the storms of life. We must become one as His trees. We must reside in His forest. With that strength, a person becomes a tree of a different sort. A tree removed from the other trees. You see David one must be saved. We call this salvation. Salvation is the work of the Divine to rescue a person from the ravages and wrath of this fallen forest. Without this work of the One, all trees are doomed and destined to be fallen. No tree can be straight and grow towards the sun without first becoming part of His forest. Look around you and you will find trees of many a sort. You have seen trees aslant or with one root or the many or with their trunks cleaved in two parts or the many. So many trees around in this forest and yet so few trees grow straight. You have also seen trunks of trees gnarled and decimated. There were trees both dead and dying. Those dead and dying trees were not of His forest, but still of His creation.

I had been so caught up in the teacher's explanation. I was oblivious to all around me except for him and the trees. I was taken by surprise when I heard a voice cry out from behind and away from me." You are right. You are right my friend. Don't forget what surrounds your trunk of salvation. What protects the trunk? What provides a hedge around the trunk?

He has made a remedy for our weakness and it is His strength. He considers that we are strong when we may actually be very weak. He renders to us His strength. This consideration from Him is called justification." I have heard of this term David remembered. A Sunday school teacher from my youth had the clever saying. She said that justification was just as if a person had not sinned. I thought I would use this chance to ask the about this justification. "But Sir, how is this possible? I know all my life I never have felt like I deserved any sort of thought or consideration from the Lord. I would try and try but I would fail most times. How then can I be just and be so bad."

I looked at the doctor and saw his head was nodding. He had raised his gnarled finger to point in my direction and behind me to another man who had interrupted the doctor's description of the trunk. He was pointing to an older man with a slight hunch to his back given to him from too many years carrying too heavy a burden. A balding man with a crumpled look of mismatched clothing garbed about him. He wore glasses, but like his clothing they were out of date. They were horn-rimmed and black and thickly made. His shirt and his trousers clashed in uncoordinated colors with a canvas belt holding the trousers from falling to the ground. He came toward us and with no shyness about him, he joined into the conversation. Doctor seemed not the least put out and in fact seemed to enjoy the banter. It was as if he knew the old man. In fact, he had known him. I was made privy of this fact very quickly.

"David that is exactly the point and it has to be what He has done," continued the doctor. "Though you are not just in any way, through him you become just. Justification is what He has done," for you that you cannot do for yourself. That is why for your tree trunk to be straight it is necessary that the Lord is the one who keeps and considers you straight. It is like the judge or any other person who has an opinion. The Lord's opinion, when you believe in him is to consider you just. Then your tree trunk is straight and strong and anchored by the Scripture, His word and Spirit. Your trunk is salvation and His justification encircles the trunk to be a protection and a hedge; a bark around the trunk. By the way, David this gentleman behind you is Pastor."[5] "Just call me Joe," my new acquaintance interruptedly added. "I know the teacher. Have for a long time. Doctor how are you? You are looking spry for a fellow of your years," added Joe with both a twinkle in his eye and a jump in his step. "I am perfect Joe as I know you are also. I was just trying to explain to David. Oh, by the way, this is David." Pastor Joe continued, "I know, I know. He is the reason I have come." Doctor continued, "I was telling our new friend how each tree needs to have a trunk from Him to be one of His trees. The straighter the better," he added. I found myself

---

[5] Pastor Joseph Johnson of the Churches of Christ in Christian Union.

somewhat encircled by the pair. Both men had age, but both seemed anew with an agility and spryness that was remarkable. In this way, they reminded me of the feeling and sensation I had experienced and felt when I saw, first Jack and then my father. They looked old, but they did not act old. It was clear and apparent that they had known each other for quite a while. Their friendship seemed to gravitate back and forth between the pair of old friends.

I had become the listener as they would verbally spar back and forth explaining some aspect of salvation or the trunk in comparison to the bark of justification. I finally, after a bit of time drifted a little from the attention I should have been giving to the pastor and the doctor. I interrupted my thought and thought a new thought for just a second or so. That seemed such an unusual term, time. It was if that time meant very little if anything in this forest. As the colors of the sky and the greens of the land and the smells and the crispness of the air were more than I had remembered before the forest, time seemed to transcend and be more than the normal and the usual. But given my lack of any other term I needed to use it.

I found myself drawn away from my private thought and was again listening intently to their instruction. I finally, after a bit of time began to understand a tad of what Doctor and Pastor were saying and explaining. The two, justification and salvation went together. Like the trunk of the tree and the bark of the tree. Justification was given by the Lord. It was Grace. Salvation was the work of the Lord. It was Grace. The Lord had accomplished the work for anyone to be saved from wrath. A saved person is deemed and considered to be just by He, Himself.

Captured by their conversation, it became more and more so that I was growing in my depth of understanding. I knew that was why I was in this forest. Jack and Dad and Doctor and Pastor Joe the Missionary were here to help and guide me to a truth. All four were to guide me through the travail of this trek. They all had told me, but like all things truth had to come to a person in experience as well as by knowledge. I think that this thought about coming to a truth hit me in both my heart and head at this moment. The light switch clicked on to a greater degree inside of me. Doctor would offer some point of salvation. Pastor would offer another point concerning justification or the vice versa. Every now and then I would hear one or the other include me and say, "You see David," or "Do you understand David?" I would nod my head not wishing to interrupt the flow of thoughts and insights offered by the two. I felt so good. Was that the correct word? I think it was. I felt so good and comfortable and at peace listening to the doctor and the missionary explaining to the novice. Each in his way and manner, but both dedicated to show some of His truth to me.

I had been enthralled with Jack. I was overjoyed with seeing and hearing Dad once again. Listening to Doctor and Pastor, I felt a keen and complete sense of contentment. The fog was lifting and the forest was becoming the clearer to me.

----------MORE ABOUT TREES----------

I heard his voice again. Dad was coming from the side out of the stand of trees. "But Doctor and Pastor there is more. Tell my son the more concerning the trees. Tell him of the limbs that grow from the trunk. Each limb also encircled and encrusted by bark to protect their all from the storms and the weathers of life." Both teacher and pastor looked toward my father and nodded. Both spoke the same reply to him. "We were just getting to that point Ken." To hear my father called by his name sent a flood of emotions over me. His real first name was Charles, but just everyone called him, Ken. His middle name was Kenith. It was spelled differently in his family. The thought came to me. How could these two men know my father's name? Joe looked at me and said, "Remember David, it is the forest." "Yes," Dad added. "Yes, indeed," added Doctor. "The forest indeed."

My father continued, "A tree needs roots and trunks and barks. Of course, of course, but it must have limbs to reach for the sky and to spread about and grow high. The Lord gives to each tree acts or deeds that He has accomplished for each." The doctor once again seemed to be excited by the thought of what my father was expressing and was swaying back and forth. I could tell by the increased twinkle in Pastor Joe's eyes that he also was appreciating my father's words. My father had moved toward us and was included in our small circle of conversation.

"A tree would not be complete without limbs growing up and out," Dad said. "Yes, yes," added the Doctor. "Yes indeed!" You are so right," Joe said in agreement. I was standing in a bit of awe and puzzlement thinking to myself. "Wait, wait we are anchored by the roots of Scripture and the Spirit. Our trunks are salvation. We are saved by the Son. Our salvation is hedged about by His justification given and ceded to us by Him and there is more?" As if right on cue, I heard Dad say, "There is more. Our limbs, these acts of Grace by Him provide fullness to our tree. They all prepare and ready the tree for the added leaves and fruits of His Spirit which must grow from the limbs.

Look about you David? See those trees there?" He pointed here and there and all around. All of the healthy trees demonstrate a good grouping of limbs don't they?" "Why yes Dad they do." "Of course," offered both Doctor and Pastor in agreement. "Well," Dad continued, "Those are the limbs you can see from far off. They provide the fullness of the tree in the tree's growth and life in the forest. They are the acts of Him and given by Him, but they are demonstrated in each tree as necessary and as accepted by each tree." My head began to swim around my father's pond of explanation. He sensed his last statement might have been a bit much for me. It had been. He stopped and let my thoughts grab ahold to his words. We all were silent for a time. "There was the word again," I thought to myself. I smiled and I chuckled out loud a wee bit.

My chuckle brought the pondering silence to a stop. All three men looked at me. I said, "Oh, forgive me. A thought came to my mind. Please Dad go on. I think I can handle a bit more." All of us chuckled together. Doctor added, "It is a parcel to gather and hold on to, isn't it David?" "Yes it is for sure," I replied.

"As I was saying," Dad continued, "The limbs grow from the trunk of the tree. They are the acts of grace by which the Lord gives to each tree for its complete development and maturity." " A tree cannot be full without its top," quipped Pastor Joe. "Must have a covering, a top," agreed the doctor. "Ahem," pronounced Dad clearing his throat. "The acts are given by the Lord. They can be many and varied. The Lord gives His redemption: the act of grace to purchase us from our sin. He gives us His propitiation: the act of grace given in order that we can be reconciled to God. He gives us His sanctification: the act of grace given which is the process of becoming holy; of becoming like He is." "But Dad," I interrupted," "How can we be holy?" "That is why these many things are given by the Lord. They are acts done by the Lord on our stead. On our behalf until we in our eternity, we will have them as part of our eternal nature. Someday we will be eternally redeemed. Someday we will be eternally reconciled. Someday we will be eternally holy. These acts of grace can also be faith and peace and repentance and righteousness and glory and regeneration. The list goes on and on David, but these I have mentioned are both examples and really, really necessary and important ones. In fact David, the list is quite innumerable as we are so fallen and imperfect, but loved and cherished by Him. We all fall short in so many things and necessities while we are in our mortality and the Lord is so gracious, if we believe in Him that He gives to us what we cannot have by our mortal natures."

"So the limbs of our trees," I spoke trying to grasp the deeper meanings of what Father had said, "Are given as acts by the Lord to us if we accept them to complete us for His use?" "Exactly," all three said together and in unison. They all looked at the others and all smiled a smile of knowledge and contentment.

My head was still swimming around in that deep lake in which I had been hurled by these three men. I was making a start of headway. I pondered a bit and the visual image of the tree began to emerge in my thoughts. I saw a tree growing from the ground of mortality. It grew from the earth anchored into the ground by two strong roots. The trunk was encompassed about by a bark to protect its trunk from the storms of life. From this trunk now grew limbs of differing proportions and lengths and diversities. More trees grew about me. Each of the trees in my mind's eye differed from the other in many ways. Some were straighter. Some were more atilt. Some had more limbs. Some had even had one larger root and the other smaller. Some were all jagged about with multiple roots or trunks divided by a cleft of multiple trunks. The dawn of understanding started to penetrate my dense brain and the instruction and education of these three good teachers began to take firmness. There were several of the trees in my mind's eye that were straight and true and sure and anchored and complete.

"It is this life," I almost screamed in a loud voice. "It is this life we live," I continued. "The forest is life and each tree is a person. I thought I knew this from the start. Jack and all of you said as much in your description. I think I understand better. We all have the opportunity and call to be one of His trees. Many don't. Those trees fallen and lying rotten and ruined about here and there all over the forest. Many trees have accepted His offer, but in their growth have strayed from His plan and program. Some have tried to add to His roots of the Scripture and the Spirit with some additional thought or scheme and thus making the tree unstable. Some have veered to one root more than the other. Preferring the Scripture and ignoring the Spirit or vice versa and thereby creating a lean or a slant and not allowing the proper balance for the tree."

I was so caught up in my dissertation I was almost ignoring my three mentors as they with smiles on their faces and nodding their heads listened to my talk. "The trunks of each tree must be the trunk of salvation. None of the acts can be considered part of the trunk. Our walk with the Lord begins with His salvation given to us if we believe and confess. I see the skewed trees here and there with cleaved trunks. Trunks displaying that a particular tree has tried to add an act of grace as a part of their trunk. The work of grace, salvation, our trunk must grow and from this trunk His acts will grow forth and up and about to cover each tree. Each trunk must be encircled by His bark of justification. Each limb also is encircled with His justification. We being unjust in our mortality must have His justness rendered to us. Given by the Lord, justification makes us just according to His reckoning and not our actions." I gazed about me and noticed in this clearing of trees an understanding concerning the limbs. Each tree had varying limbs. I knew that this was right and correct. Each tree was a different tree all growing into a Lord's tree. Some had this need. Some had this ability. Some had this deficiency. The Lord would give to each tree its need to add or enhance that particular tree. All of the trees needed the big limbs of redemption and propitiation and righteousness and holiness and the like, but the little and smaller limbs were also present with each tree. Unique to each tree and given specifically to each tree as needed. Some perhaps I should say many of the trees were not quite right in regards to the perfections in my mind. There were a few though that were growing straight and true. Each grounded into the good ground by the two proper roots.

Trunks and limbs encircled by a healthy bark. The tree's limbs growing out from and for each tree in a most beautiful manner. They were the good trees. My mind and my spirit knew this was the case.

I was reveling in my thought picture when I saw Dad and Joe and Doctor turn their gaze from me. They turned a bit of a military flank and the three looked up the hill. I could not help but also turn to face what or who they were looking at. There he was again. My friend Jack was there up the hill a bit more. "Well, well, are you going to stay there all the day?" The others just shook their heads and with a grin from ear to ear started towards Jack. Jack was waving us to come. I started up that hill towards Jack with Dad and Joe and Doctor. "We have a bit more to talk of," Jack added.

I knew his last comment was directed to me and not to the other three. "You have seen much on your trek. Your tree so far is growing and looms large, but it is still not complete. Come David look at these trees and see a little more," Jack was speaking and pointing to a stand up the hill and before our group.

"Look there." I took my cue from him and looked at a grove of the most beautiful and lush trees. The trees were perfect and from their limbs grew such foliage of leaves. I had not noticed the leaves on the other trees so far on my journey. Perhaps it just wasn't time for me to notice them. "Aye, aye," continued Jack. "You see the leaves now don't you David," as if to confirm my previous lack of insight concerning the leaves? The leaves growing from the trees have a purpose. Leaves feed and water each tree. They receive and draw energy from the sun. I should say to correct myself, the Son." The three men grinned at Jack's clever pun. I found myself content and also smiled at his reference to the Lord. "You see son a tree must be fed and watered and given energy. The roots of each tree give much, but the Lord also gives these things by the leaves. These are the gifts of the Spirit as they are referred to by many. They promote the health of each tree. They have an additional purpose in addition to these other functions. They promote the production of the fruits of each tree. If a tree is not fed or watered or has no energy, the tree's fruit will be such a pitiful and paltry demonstration of the tree that the fruit might indeed be a failure."

By the time Jack had finished speaking, the four of us had reached him on the hill. He nodded to us and turned in a twirl of sorts and without any directing word starting walking up the grade. The others started following him. I also started up the hill. We were going up and closer to the lovely trees with flowering foliage of leaves. Following Jack, we soon were near the top of the hill. Jack went off the path and started toward and into the stand of trees.

We stood there in the glade with the trees about us near and far. Jack, Pastor Joe, Dad, and Doctor stood in a bit of a semi-circle looking at me. I just stood in a bit of awe at these four men. The philosopher, the missionary, my father, and my teacher all stood in comfort and contentment. In but a short while, they had led me far into this strange forest. I remembered the gnarled tree at the beginning. I compared it and Jack's description of it early on to the trees in this glade up the hill.

Then the four turned about and just stared at the grove. I also started looking in that direction. It was much like when you see a person staring at the sky and you feel compelled to also look in that direction. I could not help myself. I stood there and was enraptured by the sights. The mighty and straight trees growing up toward the sun and sky appeared to be many, many feet high. Anchored so firmly without stagger or slant by two mighty roots. The trunk covered by the bark growing into limbs. From each of the limbs, leaves sprouting drawing moisture and nurture and food for each of the trees. Here on the hill and in this perfect of glades, these trees seemed perfect and complete in themselves. I was a bit transfixed when I saw more.

From the limbs and by the leaves I saw budding fruit. It did not take much time. "There was that pesky word again," I chided myself. The fruit seemed and appeared to grow into such beautiful and complete fruit. My four guides started to raise their hands in a type of wave. Their raised hands went first the one way and then the other. I heard the four speak words of praise to the Son, the Lord. The gloriousness of their words enthralled me to my core. They were praising the Son for the growing of the fruit from the various trees in this most perfect of groves. They praised the Spirit for His guidance and help. They praised the Father for His plan. They praised the Trinity in their mercy, grace, and love. The fruit, their fruit grew the more.

Jack, and the others turned while still waving their hands and uttering their words of praise. I, in turn felt compelled and encouraged to join them. The five of us: the philosopher, the father, the teacher, the missionary, and least of all the student, me stood in a cooperative community of worship.

In the midst of our praise, I saw something I could not believe. Each of the fruit, when they were of such a size as to be ready, fell from the trees. Each took a bit of a flight from the tree from which they grew. In a quick moment, not in any way natural, but perfectly acceptable in this forest a sapling tree started to grow. All fruit must begin their own path to become a tree in their own right.

My four companions stopped in their praise and worship and were consumed by the sight. Their stillness was in fact a type of praise in itself. I was still in awe by the proceedings. Jack in the most expressive manner, waved his arms about and shouted, "Blessed is the name of the Lord." The four men together shouted, "Blessed is the name of the Lord." I also soon could not help, but to join their chorus and shouted, "Blessed is the name of the Lord." Jack who seemed to take the lead after the chorus had finished spoke, "David do you see?" The other three men stood about smiling and nodding and waving their arms. Jack continued, "David can you see? The perfect tree when grown by the Lord and accepting the Lord's direction cannot help but grow good fruit. These trees are the trees that reflect the Son. The more each tree reflects the Son the more their fruit will be healthy and grow into good trees."

I looked at Jack with his crumpled coat and foreign speech and knowledgeable way. I looked at Doctor with his white mane of hair and his slight build. I looked at Pastor Joe with the twinkle in his eye. I looked at my father with his love in his heart and strength in his hands. I knew. I knew the message. I felt at peace. I knew what the reality apart was meant to be and above the mortal reality before my time in the tree stand. I could now see as things should be. I raised my hands to praise the Lord and a great flood of light began to encompass the glade.

I saw the great and the small of the believing people grow from what once were the trees. Amazingly, each tree was now beginning to reform as people. From all around the forest, those trees which were straight began to become people. I twirled and turned and the light began to spread from each direction of the forest.

The people started to come toward the hill. There was now in the midst of my four friends a greater tree. A tree by which all other trees would and should be judged was in the middle of all the forest. This most perfect tree began to change in my sight and mind. He became the perfection of all the forest. There on top the hill and in the midst of the forest, stood my Lord. The Lord stood in the most blinding of the light. It in fact, seemed to radiate from Him, but also gravitate towards Him. The light also seemed to cover and clothe Him in a perfection which I knew could be but His own holiness.

The light that came from the Lord surrounded at first and then covered my guides. The light was consuming all the trees, the believers throughout this forest and finally in this glade. Like a fog from the land of the hills, the light swallowed first the doctor and then Joe and Jack and finally, my father from my sight. A simple part of my thoughts first felt a tinge of alarm and then a wave of comfort. How could anyone feel loss when his guides were completely within the will and being of the Lord?

The light, His light was nearly to me. I was becoming covered by His light. I was now more and more consumed and encompassed by the clothing of His light. I was becoming complete in Him. The peace I felt. I looked about and the light came nearer to covering me in my entirety. I raised my arms to welcome His light I . . .

----------HOME AGAIN----------

I . . . "What," I shouted, "The light." Suddenly the light was gone from me. The clap of thunder woke me in the midst of the storm. I whirled about and saw only the dark of my hallway before me as I lay by the door jamb near my bed. I seemed to have fallen from my bed during the night. Whatever had happened during the night the light was gone. He, my Lord was gone from my sight. Jack and Joe and Doctor and Dad were not here. I saw no light, but only the dark foreboding of the place where I had begun my adventure during the storm. I saw no trees, but only the crack of lightning framed within the window.

My heart beat at a pace that seemed about to explode. My sweat dropped from my head and from my body as if I had malaria and my fever was breaking. I was in such a way. I was still, in my heart and mind, within the forest. I knew that in this place we called reality I was back in my home after being roused by the storm. I grabbed my robe to use as a comforter. I was by the door jamb of my bedroom. Through the course of my trial and time, I had not made it from my bedroom into the hallway that led to the front of my house. I looked about my room and found my comforter lying on the floor next to my bed. I must have not awakened during the night. My journey in the forest was a dream.

I looked out my bedroom window and noticed the storm was lessening. The claps of thunder came with a growing interval. The frequency of the lightning grew less thus making the dark sky less and less formidable. I saw a few bolts of lightning and heard the last of the claps of thunder and knew the storm was blowing over. I looked more closely through the window and saw the reddish morning sun breaking through the dark of the night coming from the east heralding a new morning. "What a dream," I called out as if to reassure someone from a fright. I was alone. The storm was frightening to me. Of course, but I felt more. I was calling out to myself. The storm had passed, but the truth of the dream stayed with me. I missed the forest. I missed Dad and my other guides. My aloneness was also from my heart and not only my condition in my bedroom. The night's dream did not flee my mind and heart like so many of the other dreams I have had. My reassurance was not relief from a fear as from the storm, but from the comfort and contentment which I found present within me as well as the yearning of their company. I had contentment in my aloneness. "This duality was a very strange one", I thought to myself.

My heart began to calm from the storm and the difference of the dream. My sweats began to subside from the storm and the exertion of both body and soul. My dream however, stayed in my mind. I grabbed my comforter and covered myself over my robe. I stood for a time in my room trying to grasp that point of life where the reality and the dream collided together. I did not bother to cover the bed with the comforter. I needed it much more than some societal convention. I thought to myself how my mother would have scolded me for this lapse. Even in my state, I found this thought comforting and funny. I sighed a smile.

All of the sudden, I heard the knocking on my door. It was more of a pounding. I would not have been surprised to hear the shout of a policeman or some other authority demanding entrance. I left my room and went through the hallway to my front door. I looked through the panes of glass and saw Dr. Alton. I must have been a sight as I opened my door. The interruption of the storm and the intensity of the dream had driven from my mind the chores of this new day.

"Ah, Doctor. Please come in, come in." I encouraged my friend and my teacher. I saw him standing there. A bit rained upon from his travel from his car in those last drops of rain. I think what I saw most was his look at bewilderment at his young student standing before him. It was one of those moments when I knew what he was thinking. I started to chuckle. "I know. I know I must look a sight." I could only imagine my appearance. I dressed in my robe and further gowned by my comforter must have looked like a refugee on some sort of a news program.

"Well, David you do look a bit worse for wear," Dr. Alton responded. "Did you forget I was to give you a ride into the town? We were to have breakfast together. I even brought you some homemade bread from my wife, Delois. I know you love her bread."

I could but stand there in my disarray. I muttered something about my long night. I stumbled out an apology, "I'm sorry Doctor... Sorry, I will hurry. It will only take a moment." Dr. Alton smiled his smile and replied, "That's all right David. Take your time, but do hurry," he laughed and came into the hallway on his way to the living room. I whirled away and hurriedly walked back to my bedroom.

In but the briefest of times, though it seemed like a forever to me, I was washed and dressed and making my way back from the bedroom to the living room.

"Well, I am set to go Doctor." "Ah, good," he replied. "Good. Let's be off. I am getting hungry," he responded with a lilt in his voice suggesting that he was starving. I laughed back at his comment. I grabbed my bag that served me as a carrying case and we both went through the door onto my front porch.

The air was refreshed from the cleansing presence of the storm and in the storm's aftermath, the sky and all around the house seemed renewed. Standing and marveling at this happening, I looked at my yard and close by the hill that led down to the forest past I saw a precious sight I had not seen before. There was a sapling. I thought to myself the where and why of this. I did not remember it there before, but this morning of all mornings there it was. A sapling of a tree was growing straight and true from the ground of my yard. I could but breathe a breath of contentment and peace as a smile formed on my face. I prayed to myself that my tree would grow straight and true and be anchored in Him.

A MIGHTY TREE – THE SERMON

On a hill far away
Stood an old rugged cross
The emblem of suff'ring and shame,
And I love that old cross
Where the dearest and best
For a world of lost sinners was slain.

On, that old rugged cross
So despised by the world,
Has a wondrous attraction for me,
For the dear Lamb of God
Left His glory above,
To bear it to dark Calvary.

To the old rugged cross
I will ever be true,
Its shame and reproach gladly bear;
Then He'll call me someday
To my home far away,
Where His glory forever I'll share.

So I'll cherish the old rugged cross,
'til my trophies at last I lay down
I will cling to the old rugged cross,
And exchange it someday for a crown.[6]

---

[6] The Old Rugged Cross, by George Bennard.

From The Good Tree

The life of the Christian, of any Christian is a life of growth and development. It is a life of submission and service. It is a life of application and adherence. This fact is true for all growth. It is especially true for the life and growth of the Christian. The word Christian means little Christs. As He is, we must become. We must pattern ourselves into a form as He would have us. This growth and development at times can be painful. The pain and the arduous nature of the task are directly connected with our stubborn natures wishing to rebel and fight the form in which He would have us. The form which He desires and commands for us, which in the final and eternal sense is His form. We read in His word through the pen of the Apostle Paul in the Letter to the Ephesians 2:7-10:

> . . . That in the ages to come He might show the exceeding riches of His grace in His kindness toward us in Christ Jesus. For by grace you have been saved through faith, and that not of yourselves; it is the gift of God, not of works, lest anyone should boast. For we are His workmanship, created in Christ Jesus for good works, which God prepared beforehand that we should walk in them.[7]

I love this portion of Scripture. In verse 10, we read the word, workmanship. That English word comes from the Greek word, *poema*. That is the word from where we

---

[7] All Scripture given in this sermon narrative are from the New King's Version of the Holy Bible.

receive the English word, poem. It is something that has been crafted and beautifully made. We are to be the poem of the Lord. We, as Christians or little Christs are to be fashioned by Him into somebody that is made and created into a form as dictated by the author, the Lord. We are to be a beautiful form fashioned by the Creator God.

Further in His word, we read in the Gospel of Matthew 22:34-41, in response to the questions proffered by those opposed to Jesus Christ as to what is the greatest commandment?

> But when the Pharisees heard that He had silenced the Sadducees, they gathered together. Then one of them, a lawyer, asked His a question, testing Him, and saying, "Teacher, which is the great commandment in the Law?" Jesus said to him, "'You shall love the Lord your God with all your heart, with all your soul, and with all your mind.'[8] This is the first and great commandment. And the second is like it: 'You shall love your neighbor as yourself."[9] On these two commandments hang all the Law and the Prophets."

This portion of Scripture aligns the believer into the order from which and by which the Lord would have us sort our priorities. The most important aspect, criterion for the believer is 'to love God." From this beginning and start, all else in the Christian's life must flow. The second priority is, 'to love your neighbor', to love your fellow-man.

---

[8] Deuteronomy 6:5.
[9] Leviticus 19:18.

This depiction of our priorities gives to us our marching orders. It tells the believers the pecking order for his considerations. These two commandments covering both the Old Testament and the teaching of the Lord in His earthly ministry in the New Testament also give to us an image, a picture for us to grab hold and etch into our mind's eye. I see a picture of the cross of the Lord. I see the vertical beam of our love to God and the horizontal beam like unto the first, but secondary in priority demonstrating our love to each other. The Lord in His death, burial, and resurrection from His passion at Calvary and the Tomb must paint a picture and create an image in our minds, our souls, and our hearts.

This priority must be our Gospel message through which we reach the world and communicate the necessity of the fact of the need of salvation and opportunity given through the passion of the Lord.

This message of the demonstration of the Gospel is further shown by the Lord in the Apostle Paul's first letter to the Corinthian Church 15:1-4:

> Moreover, brethren, I declare to you the gospel which I preached to you, which also you received and in which you stand, by which also you are saved, if you hold fast that word which I preached to you – unless you believed in vain. For I delivered to you first of all that which I also received: that Christ died for our sins according to the Scriptures, and that He was buried, and that He rose again the third day according to the Scriptures.

Keeping in mind that mental picture of the two commandments, let us delve deeper into this Grace given by God to us, His fallen creation.

I wrote earlier of the vertical and the horizontal aspects of the cross. How that vertical aspect was the love we are to have for God and the horizontal aspect was to show the love we have for each other. I maintain these two aspects intersect in demonstration of the cross of the Lord. He, Jesus Christ, God the Son loved God the Father in obedience unto His death. He loved each and every one of us, whether saved or unsaved in sacrifice unto His death. From this tree of His cross, our seed of Christian growth and life must fall to die again and be reborn into His image and His form. We must first die and then be buried and then grow forth from the tomb of our mortality like any other seed. Our seed must grow and keep growing until we can eternally be in His presence.

The Good Seed

From the good tree that is His cross and death and resurrection, we are the good seed. We read in the Gospel of Luke 9:4-8:

> And when a great multitude had gathered, and they had come to Him from every city, He spoke by a parable: "A sower went out to sow his seed. And as he sowed, some fell by the wayside; and it was trampled down, and the birds of the air devoured it. Some fell on rock, and as soon as it sprang up, it withered away because it lacked moisture. And some fell among thorns, and the thorns sprang up with it

and choked it. But others fell on good ground, sprang up, and yielded a crop a hundredfold." When He had said these things He cried, "He who has ears to hear, let him hear!"

The Lord in verse 15 of the same chapter explains what and who the good seed are:

> "But the ones that feel on the good ground are those who, having heard the word with a noble and good heart, keep it and bear fruit with patience."

We could have written on the various seeds of which the Lord speaks, but let us consider for this short exercise only the good seed. We notice that the good seed must come from the good fruit of the good tree. Our seed comes from the fruit from His tree. Our pedigree and heritage is perfect as it comes from the Perfect One. If we stay true to His message of which His tree of the cross and His resurrection has given, we will be a good fruit and have the good seed.

A second point concerning our good seed is that, as written before in this essay, our good seed must die to this world in order to live again. We read in the Apostle Paul's letter to the Romans 6: 1-11:

> What shall we say then? Shall we continue in sin that grace may abound? Certainly not! How shall we who died to sin live any longer in it? Or do you not know that as many of us as were baptized into Christ Jesus were baptized into His death? Therefore we were buried with Him through baptism into death, that just as Christ was raised from the dead by the glory of the

> Father, even so we also should walk in newness of life. For if we have been united together in the likeness of His death, certainly we also shall be in the likeness of His resurrection, knowing this, that our old man was crucified with Him, that the body of sin mighty be done away with, that we should no longer be slaves of sin. For he who has died has been freed from sin. Now if we died with Christ, we believe that we shall also live with Him, knowing that Christ, having been raised from the dead, dies no more. Death no longer has dominion over Him. For the death that He died, He died to sin once for all; but the life that He lives, He lives to God. Likewise you also, reckon yourselves to be dead indeed to sin, but alive to God in Christ Jesus our Lord.

Our seed must die in order to live again in the pattern of the Lord. Our form must transform by the conforming to His form. We read further in the Apostle Paul's letter to the Colossians 1:15-23:

> He is the image of the invisible God, the firstborn over all creation. For by Him all things were created that are in heaven and that are on earth, visible and invisible, whether thrones or dominions or principalities or power. All things were created through Him and for Him. And He is before all things, and in Him all things consist. And He is the head of the body, the church, who is the beginning, the firstborn from the dead, that in all things He may have the preeminence. For it pleased the Father that in Him all the fullness should dwell, and by Him to

> reconcile all things to Himself, by Him, whether things on earth or things in Heaven, having made peace through the blood of His cross. And you, who once were alienated and enemies in your mind by wicked works, yet now He has reconciled.

We were created through Him and for Him. We consist in Him. We are reconciled through His cross. Our fruit in which our seed from His tree resided must start with His pattern and fall from His tree. No other tree or form or pattern will suffice when we speak and refer to the eternal plan of God.

The Apostle Paul continues in this letter chapter 2: 6-10:

> As you therefore have received Christ Jesus the Lord, so walk in Him, rooted and built up in Him and established in the faith, as you have been taught abounding in it with thanksgiving. Beware lest anyone cheat you through philosophy and empty deceit, according to the tradition of men, according to the basic principles of the world, and not according to Christ. For in Him dwells all the fullness of the Godhead bodily; and you are complete in Him, who is the head of all principality and power.

We are Christians and we are to be Christ like. We are complete in Him. We, as believers, need no other. We are fully provided for in this matter through our Lord through His passion, burial, and resurrection. Our seed from our fruit and therefore, our tree must be like and imitate Him. We are complete in Him.

Our Barked Trunk

As from an acorn, a mighty oak may grow. From the good seeds from the Lord, we as believers may grow into a mighty tree to glorify Him. A tree imitating His cross: His death, burial, and resurrection. The base of the tree is its trunk. The roots attach and nourish and water the trunk. The limbs grow from the trunk. The trunk of our spiritual tree is Salvation. In this age of grace, we are saved by our belief and confession in the Lord Jesus Christ's death, burial, and resurrection. We read in the Apostle Paul's first letter to the Corinthian Church 15:1-4:

> Moreover, brethren, I declare to you the gospel which I preached to you, which also you received and in which you stand, by which also you are saved, if you hold fast that word which I preached to you – unless you believed in vain. For I delivered to you first of all that which I also received: that Christ died for our sins according to the Scriptures, and that He was buried, and that He rose again the third day according to the Scriptures.

In Romans 10:8-13, we read:

> But what does it say? "The word is near you, in your mouth and in your heart" (that is the word of faith which we preach): that if you confess with your mouth the Lord Jesus and believe in your heart that God has raised Him from the dead, you will be saved. For with the heart one believes unto righteousness, and with the mouth confession is made unto salvation. For the

Scripture says, "Whoever believes on Him will not be put to shame." For there is no distinction between Jew and Greek, for the same Lord over all is right to all who call upon Him. For whoever calls on the name of the Lord shall be saved."

Additionally, we read in Romans 8:15:

For you did not receive the spirit of bondage again to fear, but you received the Spirit of adoption by whom we cry out, "Abba, Father." The Spirit Himself bears witness with our spirit that we are children of God, and if children then heirs – heirs of God and joint heirs with Christ, if indeed we suffer with Him, that we may also be glorified together.

Without a trunk there is no tree. Without salvation there is no saved believer. This work is done by the Lord through His death, burial, and resurrection.

Our trunk of salvation and the subsequent limbs are covered by a protective bark. This is the act of grace done by the Lord which we call Justification.

Justification is a judicial act. The Lord, our sacrifice and also our judge and also our paraklete or advocate decrees that we are just. Now in this life none of us are just, but the Lord considers that we are. The fullness and completeness of His grace is so wonderful and merciful. This decree protects our trunk of salvation from the weathering and advances of the storm of mortality that assail each of us in this temporary stage of life. We in our mortality are just passing through on our way to eternity, but life is a hard life, a stormy and tempestuous life. As our trunk is encircled and protected by the bark so our salvation is surrounded and protected by His justification. We read in Romans 2:15-16:

> . . . Who show the work of the law written in their hearts, their conscience also bearing witness, and between themselves their thoughts accusing or else excusing them) in the day when God will judge the secrets of men by Jesus Christ, according to my gospel.

We further read in Romans 3:25-26:

> . . . Whom God set forth as a propitiation by His blood, through faith, to demonstrate His righteousness, because in His forbearance God had passed over the sins that were previously committed, to demonstrate at the present time His righteousness, that He might be just and the justifier of the one who has faith in Jesus.

The Lord has saved us, but He additionally, has protected us. He also has made provision to nourish and water and anchor each of our trees with His mighty roots.

Our Roots

With the first germinating of our seed, a mighty miracle starts to occur. We start to develop a root system. In my very natural and limited metaphor, I believe that the Christian tree, in its perfecting and growth will develop two roots. All trees must have a root system. The roots of any plant or tree provide nourishment and water to the tree.

This situation is also true for the Christian tree. The first root of our tree is the root of Scripture. The Holy Bible is the Word of God. We find it is the communication by the Communicator, Jesus Christ. We read in the Gospel of John 1:1-3 and 1:14:

> In the beginning was the Word, and the Word was with God, and the Word was God. He was in the beginning with God. All things were made through Him, and without Him nothing was made that was made. In Him was life, and the life was the light of men. . .And the Word became flesh and dwelt among us, and we beheld His glory, the glory as of the only begotten of the Father, full of grace and truth.

The word, 'Word,' quoted in the passage above is the Greek word, *logos,* It is the noun form for the Greek word: to speak, *lego.* It can mean word, but also reason or argument in the good sense of the word. Jesus Christ is not only the Creator God, which He is, but He is the Communicator of the Triune God. He is Scripture. He not only creates our tree. He not only provided that we can become trees in His image, but He also speaks to His own through the Scripture. Dr. Ravi Zacharias has a motto for his ministry.[10] It is "What I believe in my heart must make sense in my mind." What a wonderful thought.

The knowledge that He is not only the Creator God, but also the ebb and flow for us as believers is added by the following passages.

---

[10] Dr. Ravi Zacharias, Christian Missionary and Alliance Minister, Christian Apologist, and founder of the Ravi Zacharias International Ministries.

God, who at various times and in various ways spoke in time past to the fathers by the prophets, has in these last days spoken to us by His Son, whom He has appointed heir of all things, through whom also He made the worlds; who being the brightness of His glory and the express image of His person and upholding all things by the word of His power, when He had by Himself purged our sins, sat down at the right hand of Majesty on high, having become so much better than the angels as He has by inheritance obtained a more excellent name than they. The Letter to the Hebrews 1:1-4.

In the beginning God created the heavens and the earth. The earth was without form, and void; and darkness was on the face of the deep. And the Spirit of God was hovering over the face of the waters. Then God said, "Let there be light"; and there was light. Genesis 1:1-3.

When we read these three passages cited above together, we have the attestation, the authority to proclaim that Jesus Christ is the Word of God, Scripture. We can rest and be assured that He speaks to us and will nourish and water us with His truth. Our trees can grow straight and true to continue our metaphor anchored in His word as our root.

Our second root works in conjunction with the first root, Scripture, the Word of God, and the communications of God the Son, Jesus Christ our Lord. This second root is the Holy Spirit. The Spirit always directs us as believers toward the word and light of God the Son, re. The Gospel of John chapter 14. In this Age of Grace, the Spirit guides and educates and prepares the Bride of Christ, the Church to grow and be a chaste Bride for the Groom, the Lord. As Jesus is our *parakletos*, our comforter and advocate, so the Holy Spirit is the second *parakletos*. When God the Son ascended back to God the Father, God the Spirit came to reside within each believer.

In The Acts of the Apostles 2:1-4, we read:

> When the Day of Pentecost had fully come, they were all with one accord in one place. And suddenly there came a sound from heaven, as of a rushing mighty wind, and it filled the whole house where they were sitting. Then there appeared to them divided tongues, as of fire, and one sat upon each of them. And they were all filled with the Holy Spirit and began to speak with other tongues, as the Spirit gave them utterance.

Even in the Kingdom economy of this event and with the fulfillment of another High Holy Day of Israel by God Pentecost, the Holy Spirit has now come to fill the believers.

In the Grace Age economy we see the continued working of the Spirit within the believer in conjunction with the other two persons in our Triune God in Ephesians 1:1-14, but specifically in the following two verses concerning the Holy Spirit, written by the Apostle Paul in his letter to the Ephesians 1:13-14:

> In Him you also trusted, after you heard the word of truth, the gospel of your salvation; in whom also, having believed, you were sealed with the Holy Spirit

of promise, who is the guarantee of our inheritance until the redemption of the purchased possession, to the praise of His glory.

The Greek word translated 'guarantee', is the word, *arrabos*. Its meaning is: a pledge or a promise. It, in the modern sense, can mean: an engagement ring. I like this thought. The Holy Spirit is our engagement ring with the Triune God until we are married to the Son. He is the pledge until we have our eternality in the presence of the Holy God. In other translations, the Holy Spirit is described using the term 'earnest'. He is the down payment of God, so to speak, until we receive the fullness of God.

In the Apostle Paul's first letter to the Corinthian Church 12:3, we read of the harmony of the Son and the Spirit:

> Therefore I make known to you the no one speaking by the Spirit of God calls Jesus accursed, and no one can say the Jesus is Lord except by the Holy Spirit.

We find that our two roots will provide stability to each of our trees during the storms of life. We also find that our two roots will provide spiritual nourishment and water to each of us during our walk of mortality through the famine and the desert of this sinful world. The Lord's Scripture and the Holy Spirit will provide to each of His believers a steady and sure root to weather the storms of our mortality and ensure us to be present before Him when eternity comes to every one of us in our time.

Our Limbs

From the trunk of our tree, come forth our limbs. The limbs of each of our trees are the various Acts of Grace given by the Lord to strengthen and fill each of us in our walk with Him. These branches are as many and varied as each of His believers. Our limbs, the Acts of Grace, provide fullness to us and prepare and ready our tree for the both the Gifts of the Holy Spirit and the Fruits of the Holy Spirit. The following is a list of some of the shared Acts with Scriptural references, though there are many that are not mentioned due to space:

Sanctification, Romans 6:1-22

What shall we say then? Shall we continue in sin that grace may abound? Certainly not! How shall we who died to sin live any longer in it? Or do you not know that as many of us as were baptized into Christ Jesus were baptized into His death? Therefore we were buried with Him through baptism into death, that just as Christ was raised from the dead by the glory of the Father, even so we also should walk in newness of life. For it we have been united together in the likeness of His death, certainly we also shall be in the likeness of His resurrection, knowing this, that our old man was crucified with Him, that the body of sin might be done away with, that we should no longer be slaves of sin. For he who has died has been freed from sin. . . .Likewise4 you also, reckon yourselves to be dead indeed to sin, but alive to God in Christ Jesus our Lord. . . .And having been set free from sin, you became

> slaves of righteousness. . . .but now having been set free from sin, and having become slaves of God, you have your fruit to holiness, and the send, everlasting life.

Sanctification is the Act from the Lord given to the process of making each believer to be more and more holy. We all, in the eternal realm must be holy as He is holy. In our mortal state and being failed earthen vessels holding His precious salvation within us, we begin to cast off our corrupt and mortal fallen nature and become more and more like He is in His perfection. We continually, more and more are becoming a new creature. A creature growing to be patterned and holy like the Lord.

Faith, Romans 4:16:

> Therefore it is of faith that it might be according to grace, so that the promise might be sure to all the seed, not only to those who are of the law, but also to those who are of the faith of Abraham, who is the father of us all.

Faith is what a person believes to be true. The Lord helps our faith and strengthens it in order that we can more fully believe in His gospel truth. In this Age of Grace, it is that He died for our sins and was buried in holiness and rose that third day in resurrection power, 1 Corinthians 15:1-4. Faith is our part of the grace – faith interaction between God and us. Faith is also an act given by and done by the Lord to help us and give to our tree additional fullness and maturity and strength.

Peace, Romans 2:10 and 5:1:

. . . **But glory, honor, and peace to everyone who works what is good, to the Jew first and also to the Greek.**

Therefore, having been justified by faith, we have peace with God through our Lord Jesus Christ . . .

As believers, God is not mad at us. The enmity that existed from Adam's fall is resolved and reconciled by the Lord. Our sin debt is paid for by the Lord's grace. The storm of our lostness and sin has been blown from us through the mighty wind of the Lord and we now can enjoy the freshness of the clean air of His presence. He has opened His arms to greet the believers into His presence and peace. He loved us so very much that He has paid the price to give to us peace and to do away with the enmity necessary due our fall.

Regeneration (renewing), Titus 3:5 and 2 Corinthians 5:17:

. . . **Not by works of righteousness which we have done, but according to His mercy He saved us, through the washing of regeneration and renewing of the Holy Spirit.**

> Therefore, if anyone is in Christ, he is a new creation; old things have passed away; behold, all things have become new.

If our car battery is dead, we must recharge it with a charge from a power source. Regeneration = renewing = starting again. An act provided by God to His believers. We started to live when we were saved. Throughout our mortal time, we are restarted, regenerated by His word and His Spirit.

Repentance, 2 Timothy 2:25:

> ... In humility correcting those who are in opposition, if God perhaps will grant them repentance, so that they may know the truth

Making repentance an act as opposed to an instrument leading to salvation may sound a bit odd to the reader. I am dispensational and in this Age of Grace as opposed to the Kingdom Age the only work of God is Salvation. There can be no works righteousness tacked to His finished work of the cross. Repentance, *metanoio* = to change one's mind, afterthought, must grow forth from the trunk of salvation as a mighty limb. We must change our direction and our minds and put on the mind of the Lord. We must not, in this Age of Grace put our spiritual cart before our spiritual horse. Our horse is salvation and our cart, in this case is repentance.

There are many others, but here is a short listing of some of the additional Acts:

Holiness, Romans 6:19

I speak in human terms because of the weakness of your flesh. For just as you presented your members as slaves of uncleanness, and of lawlessness leading to more lawlessness, so now present your members as slaves of righteousness for holiness.

Propitiation, the act of gaining or regaining the favor, Romans 3:25:

. . . Whom God set forth as a propitiation by His blood, through faith, to demonstrate His righteousness, because in His forbearance God had passed over the sins that were previously committed.

Redemption, Romans 3:24

. . . Being justified freely by His grace through the redemption that is in Christ Jesus.

Glory, Romans 2:10

. . . But glory, honor, and peace to everyone who works what is good, to the Jew first and also to the Greek.

I have given such a short list. By no means is this listing meant to be exhaustive. The Scriptural references are, but a taste of the breadth and depth and height of His grace acting upon His believers. His grace is dimensional and all-encompassing to His believers. His acts provide the fullness to each of our trees if we are believers in Him and the grace

He has offered to whosoever will. With the maturation of the limbs of our trees, we move to the Gifts of the Spirit and the Fruit of the Spirit.

Our Leaves

The leaves that grow from the limbs, the branches of our tree, to continue our picture are the Gifts of the Holy Spirit. The leaves feed and water the tree, but they also draw energy from the Sun. These actions promote the health of the tree and to promote healthy fruit.

There is a diversity of gifts as in the same way there are a diversity of leaves. This diversity is due that each of our trees are different. They have different needs and callings thus requiring different gifts. A gift is a gift. It is given by the Holy Spirit for a purpose. They are given to equip and empower and encourage each tree to fulfill its function in the divine plan. Within Paul's first letter to the Corinthian Church 12:4–14:14, we read a long treatise concerning the gifts. Paul writes of the gifts and then clarifies that the preeminent factor in each person is love and then further modifies and amplifies his views concerning the gifts. He also writes in his letter to the Ephesians 4:11-16:

> And He Himself gave some to be apostles, some prophets, some evangelists, and some pastors and teachers, for the equipping of the saints for the works of ministry, for the edifying of the body of Christ, till we all come to the unity of the faith and of the knowledge of the Son of God, to a perfect man, to the measure of the stature of the fullness of Christ; that

> we should no longer be children, tossed to and fro and carried about with every wind of doctrine, by the trickery of men, in the cunning craftiness of deceitful plotting, but, speaking the truth in love, may grow up in all things into Him who is the head —Christ- from whom the whole body, joined and knot together by what every joint supplies, according to the effective working by which every art does its share, cases growth of the body for the edifying of itself in love.

In modern Christianity, we have made the Lord to be are personal ATM machine. We stand before Him and deposit our spiritual debit card and attempt to withdraw what we think we need. The above passage makes it clear that the church's leadership by their gifts, their leaves is to instruct the church. They are to train the church to use their gifts, leaves so that we do the ministry. That ministry is to increase the church and to mature into His image and stature. That is the purpose of the gifts of the Spirit. That is the function of our leaves on each of our trees in His forest of Christianity.

The Fruit

The end result of any healthy tree is to bear healthy fruit. That is one of the main results of our trees. In Paul's letter to the Galatians 6:22-25 we read:

> But the fruit of the Spirit is love, joy, peace, longsuffering, kindness, goodness, faithfulness, gentleness, self-control. Against such there is no law. And those who are Christ's have crucified the flesh

and its passions and desires. If we live in the Spirit, let us also walk in the Spirit. Let us not become conceited, provoking one another, envying one another.

Colossians 3:12-17:

Therefore, as the elect of God, holy and beloved, put on tender mercies, kindness, humility, meekness, longsuffering; being with one another, and forgiving one another, if anyone has a complaint against another; even as Christ forgave you, so you also must do. But above all these things put on love, which is the bond of perfection. And let the peace of God rule in your hearts, to which also you were called in one body; and be thankful. Let the word of Christ dwell in you richly in all wisdom, teaching and admonishing one another in psalms and hymns and spiritual songs, singing with grace in your hearts to the Lord. And whatever you do in word or deed, do all in the name of the Lord Jesus, giving thanks to God the Father through Him.

Romans 15:1-7, 13-14:

We then who are strong ought to bear with the scruples of the weak, and not to please ourselves. Let each of us please his neighbor for his good, leading to edification. For even Christ did not please Himself; but as it is written, "The reproaches of those who reproached you fell on Me." For whatever things were written before were written for our learning, that we through the patience and comfort of the Scriptures might have hope. Now may the God of patience and comfort grant you to be like-minded toward one another, according to Christ Jesus, that you may with one mind and one mouth glorify the God and Father of our Lord Jesus Christ. Therefore receive one another, just as Christ also received us, to the Glory of God. . . Now may the God of hope fill you with all joy and peace in believing, that you may abound in hope by the power of the Holy Spirit. Now I myself am confident concerning you, my brethren, that you also are full of goodness, filled with all knowledge, able also to admonish one another.

Our fruit will reflect our tree. If we have a healthy tree, we will reproduce like fruit.

In conclusion, our tree planted in the soil by the roots of His Word and Spirit, rises with a straight trunk through the sky of our life toward the Son. We will grow in His image as we are born of His seed. The famines of life may come, but we are fed by Him. The droughts of life may dry others, but we are watered by Him. The storms and tempests of life may howl, but we are anchored by Him and His Spirit. Our salvation is protected by His justification therefore our trees will have full limbs reaching from the trunk upward and outward. These limbs, these Acts of the Holy Spirit graciously ensure our good gifts, our leaves. This action ensures good fruit, other believers who will grow into the likeness of Jesus Christ our Lord.

GLORY, PRAISE, AND HOSANNA

When this trial of life is o'er
And I cross the river's shore
When burdens aside are laid
Through grace, the price paid
Glory to His Holy name
He who covered my shame
Praise to Jesus above
He showed me His eternal love
Hosanna for carrying the cross
He allowed me not to suffer loss
Sickness and pain not found there
I will no longer have any care
Forever I will give Him praise
Not for a time, but every eternal day
Let me always thank Him
The Redeemer of my sin
What can I give the God of renown
I can give my worker's crown
Glory and praise and hosanna
He fed me His divine manna
A poor return and it seems not fair
My crown for the defeater of evil's snare
He lived and died and lived again
The resurrection, the life, the victor o'er sin.[11]

---

[11]"Glory, Praise and Hosanna," from <u>Eclectic Essays</u>. Rev. David E. Clarke. FWB Publishing, 2011.